Senior Moments

Senior Moments

THE COMPLETE GUIDE
ON HOW
TO BE SENIOR

ANGUS FITZSIMONS

INSPIRED BY THE COMEDY REVUE *SENIOR MOMENTS*
BY ANGUS FITZSIMONS AND KEVIN BRUMPTON

hachette
AUSTRALIA

hachette
AUSTRALIA

Published in Australia and New Zealand in 2020
by Hachette Australia
(an imprint of Hachette Australia Pty Limited)
Level 17, 207 Kent Street, Sydney NSW 2000
www.hachette.com.au

10 9 8 7 6 5 4 3 2 1

A catalogue record for this
book is available from the
National Library of Australia

ISBN: 978 0 7336 4560 0 (paperback)

Cover design and illustrations by Christabella Designs
Typeset in Bembo Std Pro by Kirby Jones
Printed and bound in Great Britain by Clays Ltd, Elcograf S.p.A.

The paper this book is printed on is certified against the
Forest Stewardship Council® Standards. McPherson's Printing
Group holds FSC® chain of custody certification SA-COC-005379.
FSC® promotes environmentally responsible, socially beneficial
and economically viable management of the world's forests.

Dedication

To Julie Andrews, a great lady who had the taste and discretion not to reveal our extremely hot sexual affair.

To my wife, an extremely understanding or unobservant woman.

Oh, and to Shakespeare. It is a bittersweet moment to surpass one's hero, but if Bill were alive, I'm sure he would take it pretty well.

Denunciation

To all those who doubted me: eat it. You know who you are. I would name you, but I am still toying with the idea of hiring various hoodlums to find you and thrash you; and I don't want the cops to have an obvious link when this happens. I will make an exception in the case of Charlotte Rampling, who, unlike Julie Andrews, blabbed to everyone about her fling with me, including the story about the time I could not get the handcuffs off after she swallowed the key on purpose, which she thought was a hoot. The Hotel Manager of the InterContinental, the litigious maid who discovered me, and her subsequent Counsel thought otherwise. Thanks a bunch, Rampling. Consider yourself named; although semi-protected by the fact that I have just publicly mentioned you. And I know how you think; do not attempt to stage an accident to make it look like I did it, Charlotte, you couldn't stage a convincing revival of 'No, No, Nanette' let alone a convincing hit and run.

Table of Contents

FOURWORDS by MAX GILLIES, AM

Quadruple. Quartet. Mixed-Doubles. Quatro.

Sincerely,
Max Gillies

CHAPTER 1
Senior Moments

CONGRATULATIONS ON BEING A SENIOR! OTHER PEOPLE, LIKE James Dean and Buddy Holly, got nowhere near your achievement. And congratulations on purchasing this book, or at least stealing the copy of somebody who did.

What is a 'Senior Moment'? It can be as simple as forgetting your own address the moment you hop in a taxi, or as complicated as actually being able to remember each of Elizabeth Taylor's husbands. (Which is more than she could do. Married one twice by mistake. Welsh chap, handsome, drank like a fish, it's on the tip of my tongue... *damn*.)

Anyway, a 'Senior Moment' is a sign that Father Time is getting way too familiar with you. Here are a few you might recognise:

It's a 'Senior Moment' when...

It's a Senior Moment when you can remember being told the King was dead (George, not Elvis).

It's a Senior Moment when you still say 'Colour Television'. And you still watch television on a television.

It's a Senior Moment when you ask your travel agent why they don't have any travel packages to Ceylon. (And no direct flights to Rhodesia, either.)

1

It's a Senior Moment when you realise that you have to do five hours of yoga before you're flexible enough to do one hour of yoga.

It's a Senior Moment when you're halfway through a brilliant John Wayne impression and realise that none of the young people in the room know who John Wayne is and just think you've had a stroke.

It's a Senior Moment when you have to explain to someone what liquid paper was. And what carbon paper was. And what a newspaper was.

It's a Senior Moment when to you 'WW' means the start of a war, not an internet address.

It's a Senior Moment when you realise you've stopped worrying about dying from a drug overdose and started worrying about dying from a drug under-dose.

It's a Senior Moment when you know who Danny Kaye is but you think Kanye West is part of a country in Africa.

It's a Senior Moment when you realise it used to be the policemen who looked young, now it's the Prime Ministers.

It's a Senior Moment when you realise that your wardrobe has become ironic. You're not back in fashion, but you're hip. (And ironically, you now have an artificial hip.)

It's a Senior Moment when you know that the Ink Spots were a singing group and an indication of poor penmanship.

It's a Senior Moment if you can remember when Martina Navratilova said she liked guys and Jim Nabors said he didn't.

It's a Senior Moment when you still eat starch in the morning and use it on your shirt, too.

It's a Senior Moment when you can remember the only time you used to see a tattoo was when you were watching Hervé Villechaize on *Fantasy Island*.

It's a Senior Moment when you boast about doing it three times a night and you're just talking about getting up to pee.

It's a Senior Moment when you go bird watching with binoculars and you watch actual birds. (Although sometimes you still keep an eye out for the rare window-framed Red-Headed Strumpet).

So, these are all unquestionably Senior Moments. But *what* is the *Senior Moments* book, I rhetorically hear you ask? Well, you should have thought about that before you bought it. Other options are available. I hear *The No. 1 Ladies' Detective Agency* is pretty good, but it's too late for that now.

This book is a simple instructional guide and aide de memoire (*don't panic, this is all the French you will get in this thing*) for all Seniors on how to negotiate their way easily through Senior Life. So sit back, relax and have a read. Or stand up, be anxious and have a read. Or don't read it at all, what do I care? I've already got my cut of the royalties, happened as soon as the back of this tome blipped passed the scanner, you can burn the damn thing if you like. (Not recommended if purchased on Kindle.)

CHAPTER 2

Senior Moments at Christmas

CHRISTMAS COMES BUT ONCE A YEAR, ALTHOUGH AS A SENIOR you could swear it happened six months ago and you *will* swear if you hear Paul McCartney singing *'(Simply Having A) Wonderful Christmastime'* again, which you will, sometime in the next five minutes. Sir Paul may well be a melodic genius on par with Mozart, but when it comes to writing Christmas songs he is rubbish. (Of course, if Mozart smoked the amount of weed Sir Paul does then we're guessing that *The Marriage of Figaro* may well have ended up sounding like the theme to *The Magic Roundabout* on Mogadon, too.)

Ten Signs You Know You Are Having a Senior Christmas

1. You can remember when children had a 'Christmas Present', singular.

2. You can also remember when all the shops, no exceptions, used to close on Christmas. (No, hang on, that was called 'Sunday'.)

3. You still instinctively sit at attention at the start of the Queen's Speech.

4. You set the Plum Pudding on fire. (Not intentionally, but if you run into the dining room quickly guests will think you are 'maintaining tradition'.)

5. You insist on Bing not Bublé.

6. You are the only person qualified to do currency conversions when 'A Christmas Carol' is being read. *No, a shilling was a good tip for carrying the largest turkey in the window. Now, if it was tuppence…*

7. You keep trying to find out which TV station is showing the Morecambe and Wise special. (Or at least that Christmas episode of *The Good Life* where Margot plays charades.)

8. If anyone writes 'Xmas' you let them know 'Xactly' how irritating that is.

9. You never, ever say 'Happy Holidays'. This isn't about being happy, it's Christmas.

10. Somebody will give you a book by Peter FitzSimons. Don't fight it, it is now compulsory that everyone over 65 must be given at least one.

A Senior Christmas will usually involve your annual trip to Church. The Minister will of course "Welcome many *familiar* faces, *(pause)* and some *new ones*". No, he is not making a crack about your facelift, he is trying to make you feel guilty about only coming once a year. Well, so does Santa and everybody loves him. Get on with the children's Nativity Play and the full choir doing '*O Come, All Ye Faithful*', that's what we came for.

As Senior Church Veterans know, apart from '*All Things Bright and Beautiful*', Christmas Carols are the only upbeat Hymns ever written, which is probably the reason they are only allowed out once a year for fear the congregation might cheer up and stop coming. There is not a dud amongst them and they are great fun even for non-singers to have a go at with gusto:

'*The Holly and The Ivy*', '*God Rest You Merry, Gentleman*' and '*We Wish You a Merry Christmas*' are all belters and almost as good as proper songs. (Although we do question the latter's obsession with obtaining 'Figgy Pudding'. Have you ever tried Figgy Pudding? Dreadful. It tastes like Figs.)

Between Carols you will have to listen to the usual insights from the Minister using their special Christmastime Playschool Presenter Voice in case we *miss the point*, i.e. "A *lot* of people think that Christmas is about Holidays, or Family or Turkey or Presents. But it isn't. *(short pause)* Do *you* know what Christmas is really about? *(long pause)*... Jesus!" Try to look surprised or at least nod thoughtfully, after all it's Christmas and one should be nice to Ministers, too.

(We would point out that the Three Wise Men also thought Christmas was about presents – Gold, Frankincense, and Myrrh to be precise. Useless presents for a baby, by the way. Wise they may have been, Appropriate Shoppers they were not.)

Christmas Lunch: If still in charge of culinary matters, Seniors should not get inventive with Christmas Lunch; stick to Dry Roast Turkey, Wet Compensatory Gravy and a Ham. That's what the punters want and you should give it to them or next year you will not be able to thwart your Daughter-in-Law's dream of taking over and you will be relegated to Pudding Prep.

For the love of God do *not* be influenced by British Cooking Shows and 'try something different'. Christmas is about everything *being the same*, we are not at home to Mr Difference on the 25th of December. Oh, and on no account try 'mixing it up' with a 'Saucy Seafood Yuletide Feast'. Nigella can get away with this sort of thing because she wears tight Christmas sweaters and hypnotises anybody who might even dare say boo to her. You can't, so don't.

The Turkey: Every Senior has their own sacred turkey cooking recipe, it is a Family Tradition, reaching back into time immemorial (or 1978 to be exact when you copied Margaret Fulton's recipe out of *The Australian Women's Weekly* and pretended it was from your grandmother). Do not get neurotic about the Turkey. We have known Seniors who rise shaking with fear at dawn to continue the 4th round of re-basting before being dragged reluctantly back to bed as they scream the word 'MOIST'. This would have been sexy in your twenties, as a Senior it is a sure sign you are losing it.

Relax, it makes no difference; no matter how early you begin preparations, the Turkey will be served *at least* 45 minutes late, and it will be dryer than the Gobi Desert on a particularly brutal summer afternoon. Nevertheless, your nearest and dearest will be so sloshed that extravagant compliments will flow from them as generously as the Sav Blanc and Champers is flowing into them.

Christmas With Vegans: They can just eat Brussels Sprouts and lump it. Honestly, at least the Vegetarians eat the Mashed Potato, which is also lumpy but actually tastes nice. (And don't sulk, Vegans; Christmas is not a time for Martyrs, that is Easter.)

Mysterious Foreign Boyfriend: Every Senior Christmas will feature the late addition of a surprisingly good-looking youth in their twenties from Denmark, Sweden or Spain who is courting one of your great-nieces. (Or great-nephews, we are hip, Daddy-O.) They are perfectly harmless and will remain silent throughout the entire meal. Do not try to make conversation or it will go like this:

You: So, Björn, I suppose Christmas is very different in your country?

Endless Pause

Björn: Yes.

End of Conversation

The Mysterious Foreign Boyfriend may shriek mildly as you bring in the lit Christmas pudding, but other than that he has limited entertainment value and will be happiest if treated as an ornament.

Wearing Silly Christmas Hats: Nobody is too big, too 'grown-up' or too Senior to not wear a Silly Paper Crown Hat after pulling a cracker at Christmas Lunch. Even the Queen does it, and she has a Real Crown and wears Silly Hats practically every day. Don't be a Stuffy Senior, put it on and read aloud the Cracker Joke like a sport. *Where did Napoleon keep his armies?* Up his sleevies. (Admit it, you smiled.)

Christmas Presents: A Senior Code Guide

As a Senior you are now 'difficult to buy for'. This could be solved by the simple method of handing you cash, but for some reason your relatives never seem to think of this obvious solution. All Seniors inevitably receive a few terrible gifts; please employ the following Senior Codes in a suitably thrilled tone of voice to deal diplomatically with the disappointments.

'**Wherever did you get this?**' = Am returning tomorrow, name the shop at once

'**How *did* you know?**' = That this would displease me

'**Well, *that* is something!**' = This is a physical object

'**I *just* saw this the other day!**' = But I did not buy it for obvious reasons

'**Did you make this yourself?**' = No professional would take responsibility for this

'**This is *unique*!**' = Only a madman would have made more than one

'***So* thoughtful!**' = You did this deliberately, didn't you?

When it comes to presents, Seniors should be on the lookout for the following two recent disturbing phenomena:

1. **'Secret Santa':** The secret is that your family can't be bothered to buy you presents anymore. Secret Santa, my foot. Cheap Claus more like it. Look, we all knew the real Secret of Santa when you were children: *it was us!* We bought your presents, got no credit *and* had to chew on a carrot to pretend to be Rudolph. The least you could all do now that you have an independent income is to fork over for a pair of socks or a Celebrity Autobiography once a year.

2. **'A Donation has been recently made in your name':** Oh, really? A curse has been *very* recently made using *your* name. It's Christmas! *Give me my bloody present!* You can give a

Goat to some family overseas in your own time. (Why, one wonders, is it always a Goat? Is it a Merry Christmas for the Goat, being flown overseas to be used as a Goat Slave by some selfish family in Uganda? That Lonely Goatherd that Julie Andrews used to sing about will be even lonelier now as they stand high on the hill.)

Come to think of it, many Seniors will have noticed that the previously unheard of 'Goat Cheese' has been popping up recently on menus, be they airline or restaurant. Whether the Cheese is made from the actual Goat itself or from its milk is difficult to determine by the taste alone, which is revolting. We would rather have a second serve of Figgy Pudding.

Anyway, we suspect that all these unwanted Charity Goats and the Ugandan Cheese Industry are the reason behind this four-footed fromage fright, another sad case of unintended consequences that could have been avoided if you'd ponied up with a proper present. (And if you give a Pony to somebody next year, it had better be me.)

Senior Warning – Regifting: This is a tempting but dangerous practice for Seniors, as you often forget who gave you the unwanted gift in the first place. I know of one case of two Senior Sisters who have been exchanging the exact same copy of *The Guernsey Literary and Potato Peel Pie Society* for sixteen Christmases running.

Christmas Films

Every Senior has an obligation to make all younger relatives watch the following Senior Classics at Christmas time or it simply *will not* be Christmas. Viewing is permitted up until the end of Boxing Day:

White Christmas: with Bing Crosby, Danny Kaye and Rosemary Clooney. (And Vera-Ellen, but her nephew was not George Clooney so nobody can remember her name.) This film is indeed a Very White Christmas – the sole black character is a bartender – but it does do better than that other Christmas staple, *Holiday Inn* with Bing and Fred Astaire, which features an entire blackface number with no actual black faces in it. (Let us pray they never colourise the thing, it's barely getting away with broadcast at the moment.)

The plot of *White Christmas* is simple: Bing must sing '*White Christmas*' at least three times before a) the movie finishes and b) Danny mugs himself to death. No, it is a charming film that holds up wonderfully and you would have to have a heart of stone not to tear up at the end when (spoiler alert) the dignified but broke old General, Dean Jagger, is surprised by all of the men he once commanded in WW2, so Bing can sing '*White Christmas*' once again as it snows at last. Then Dean Jagger does a killer version of '*Jumping Jack Flash*' and the movie is over.

It's A Wonderful Life: One of the very few Christmas films to begin with an attempted suicide (an especially surprising act as '*(Simply Having A) Wonderful Christmastime*' was not written until 1978 and there is no way Jimmy Stewart could have heard the song once, let alone 4,000 times, which is usually the tipping point).

Actually, a good third of this classic film consists of Jimmy Stewart snapping at his children, complaining about how stupid everyone in town is, and glaring at his spouse. This makes the film Eternally Relatable but the beauty of the conclusion breaks every Grinch and reminds you to cheer up because everything could be a lot worse. For instance, you could be watching *Jingle All The Way* with Arnold Schwarzenegger, which your grandson was just given on VHS. That was a bloody Black Christmas indeed.

The Great Escape: Not strictly speaking a Christmas Movie, but what the hell. (If you haven't seen it before, don't get too attached to anybody except Steve McQueen or James Garner, trust us.)

CHAPTER 3
Inspiring Seniors

EVEN THOUGH SOCIETY AND YOUR G.P. BOTH THINK YOU ARE past it, you can still draw inspiration from other Seniors close to your ever-advancing age who managed to shine bright well into their twilight years.

Methuselah: Lived to the age of 969. Good innings at any time, but especially so considering this was before Medicare. Kept in shape and did not look a day over 600 when he left us. One only hopes that Methuselah was in the right Industry Based Super Fund, or those last few centuries on just the pension may have been a bit tight.

Dame Olivia de Havilland: Made it to the age of 104! This woman was in *Gone with the Wind* and dated Errol Flynn, and was still breathing in 2020! (Of course, a lot of girls '*dated*' Errol, and many of them are still suspiciously young, but she did it when he was in peak *Robin Hood* form.)

Also, stopped speaking to her sister Joan Fontaine at the Academy Awards in 1942 and they both kept up the snit until Joan carked it in 2013. Now that is Senior Grudge Holding at its finest. Dame Olivia allowed herself a brief *sotto voce* 'So there!' as the casket was lowered, but we regard both sisters' non-speaking streak as intact. When Dame Olivia passed on she was the all-time winner of the 'My God, Was She Still Alive?' award.

Frank Lloyd Wright: World's greatest architect who designed and built the Guggenheim at age 91. Not on his own, he had a couple of brawny Brooklyn fellows with hard hats helping with the non-circular bits, but still impressive. Plus, Simon and Garfunkel sang that song about him. No, not '*Mrs Robinson*', think harder. No, not '*Bridge Over Troubled Water*', he was an architect, not an engineer. You'll figure it out. So long!

Agatha Christie: Best-selling writer in history apart from Shakespeare and his murder mysteries were easy to figure out (it was usually Macbeth). Still writing annual bestsellers up until her death at the age of 86. We are not saying quality did not decrease ever so slightly; in her last few books, Hercule Poirot used to gather all the suspects together in the drawing room and ask everyone if they had seen his keys.

Still, Dame Agatha gave it a red hot go all the way, she even pre-wrote two books to be published after her death! J.D. Salinger only managed one novel when he was alive. Lazy sod.

Jane Fonda: Hanoi Jane has always been a divisive figure but one must admit that she has kept her figure. The woman is in her early 80's and still has the same waistline that she did in the early '80s. We now regret throwing out our *Jane Fonda Workout* VHS Tapes; there was obviously something in it.

Ms Fonda currently gets arrested on a weekly basis while in Washington to protest on behalf of the environment. This may sound silly, but it does help fill out her Fridays and, as Seniors know, this is one of the pre-weekend dead zones that is always a bit dull.

Winston Churchill: Became Prime Minister of England for the first time at age 74. Not really, he was 64, just looked older because he smoked like a chimney and drank like a fish. But he still managed to beat Hitler, didn't he? Churchill used to drink the alcoholic equivalent of a bottle of Scotch every day throughout World War II and he only took the cigar out of his mouth during Question Time. Tell that to the wet-behind-the-ears, straight-out-of-med-school 'physician' when they say you can only have half a glass of medicinal red wine.

Grandma Moses: She started painting at the age of 78, plus she was the grandmother of Moses (from the Bible).

The Rolling Stones: Okay, they haven't released a really good album since *Some Girls* in 1978 but they are *STILL ALIVE*. And that, as you know, is the primary aspiration of all Seniors. (We know Brian Jones is *not* still alive, but aquatic accidents do not count.)

The Queen: Has had the same job for 65 years and her children have still not managed to get her to sell her house and move into a sensible retirement home. Plus, still married to Phil the Greek who, believe you me, makes your husband look like Gandhi when it comes to good behaviour.

Pablo Picasso: Painted right up until the day he died at age 91 (including inside the lid of the casket; that man had a work ethic). Yes, some of the noses on his paintings did look a bit odd, and like you we also secretly prefer Claude Monet, but still he had a damn good innings.

Harper Lee: At the age of 89, released a sequel to *To Kill a Mockingbird* 55 years after the original classic. She showed everyone that you are never too old to disappoint your fans. Honestly, Harper, Boo Radley could have written a better follow-up than this. Still, she finished the thing, which is more than you've done with that childhood memoir you keep muttering about. Get on with it.

Joan Collins: Age indeterminant. Despite being held together entirely by wigs and make-up and the fact that she has not done anything since *Dynasty* got cancelled in the late 1980s, Dame Joan has got it going on and is still glamorous and amorous. The woman acted with Bette Davis in 1955, had Warren Beatty as a toy boy before you even knew who he was and co-starred with Bob and Bing in a 'Road' movie; how is she still alive and looking this good?

Whether it is due to a pact with the Devil or an unerring eye for quality plastic surgeons, every Senior must dip their lid to Dame Joan. She has taken Zsa Zsa Gabor's mantle of the Sexy Senior who is surprisingly super famous for reasons most people can't quite remember.

CHAPTER 4

Senior Moments in Medicine

BEFORE YOU EVEN HAVE A CHANCE TO BE MISDIAGNOSED, THE Senior must get an appointment. This used to be an easy matter, believe it or not, Youngsters; the Doctors actually used to come to your house! They also used to ask for '*hot water and towels and plenty of it*', which in retrospect makes us think they may have just been stopping in for a quick bath. Anyways, those days are gone. Nowadays, to see a physician, you have to follow one of the two basic medical Restaurant Models:

The Deli System: Turn up at the Medical Centre and take a number. There is no way on earth to know how long you will be waiting, in fact a performance of *Waiting for Godot* is often shorter and makes more sense than the G.P. when you get to the end.

You used be able to roughly work out how many people were ahead of you, but now each Medical Centre is cunningly set up like an elaborate French Farce, with a series of doors opening and closing at random times with a Doctor stepping out for a second and saying '*Mr Tibbit?*' in a tone of gentle, coaxing enquiry like a batman waking up a mildly important General during the Great War. If no answer is given, the door shuts and is not re-opened. What happened to Mr Tibbit? *Was there a Mr Tibbit?*

It is best not to think of such things, instead spend your time wisely by examining your fellow waiting patients and diagnosing them by appearance. (Yeast infection for Blondie, croup for Infant, kidney trouble for Twitchy.)

The Fully Booked System: All private medical practices behave now as though they are extremely Fashionable Restaurants. Each Doctor you enquire after is 'fully booked until next Friday'; this news delivered in a tone of faint surprise that you would have the nerve to ask in the first place. As your rash is not occurring *next* Friday but is happening *now*, which is this Monday, you, putting on your best Worried Senior Voice are reduced to begging for any availability to the Medical Maître D' who, after a sigh, might '*just be able to squeeze you in*' at the time of maximum inconvenience to your own life.

Whether you arrive at the Deli or the Fully Booked, you will notice one Waiting Room perennial is now strangely missing: the *Reader's Digest*. We used to look forward to a bit of literary slumming at the G.P. by gobbling up this extremely digestible volume, which assumed a reading level of Age 8 and employed writers who were apparently 11.

Each volume was at least two years out of date, and some were decades old, meaning you could read articles like '*What does the future hold for Princess Grace?*' and experience the morbid thrill of being able to see the future. No subject, person or book was too complicated to be condensable into five well-illustrated miniature pages by the *Reader's Digest*.

Its scope was breathtaking: a single issue from 1977 contained the articles '*After Brezhnev: A Succession Crisis?*', '*The Beguiling World of Little Known Marsupials*', '*First Aid for Ailing Marriages*', '*Do you have a Space Age Mind?*' and '*Search for the Missing Tomcat*'. (Strangely enough, the Tomcat was found in the Kremlin and briefly succeeded Andropov after he dropped off, which happened a lot to Russian leaders in the '80s. One wonders where Putin was located during this suspicious time.)

Reader's Digest also had regular features like '*Life's Like That!*' (made-up stories sent in by readers), '*Laughter: the Best Medicine!*' (not true, penicillin wins in a walk), and of course '*WordPower*' (presumably a gentle hint to the staff to consult a thesaurus occasionally).

Sadly, *Reader's Digest* is no longer being read in waiting rooms, being replaced by rather too well thumbed copies of *Woman's Day* and *New Idea*. These publications are hardly likely to be interested in searching for any missing Tomcat, unless it is dating at least one Kardashian. *Vale, Reader's Digest, we hardly knew and barely read ye.*

As Seniors grow older they must learn the important art of:

How to Lie Responsibly to Your Physician

There is a delicate balance to be observed here: you want to tell *enough* porkies to be able to keep getting the good pills, but not *so many* lies that you end up getting the good casket.

Obviously, your G.P. knows that you are going to lie, they expect nothing less from all their patients. In much the same way as when you are pulled over by the RBT and asked '*Have you had anything to drink earlier this evening?*' and you say '*I had a beer earlier*', both you and the Police Officer know this is not the full story. Unfortunately for you, the Copper has a breathalyser that can show that you did indeed have *a* beer, followed by six others in quick succession.

The G.P., unless they have an MRI machine and a lie detector test in their office (always a bad sign, but common in the Cuban

Health System), has no such precise methods to demonstrate your fibs, but the Senior should still be on guard. Your Doctor will also lie almost constantly to you; this is known as 'Bedside Manners' and is important if G.P.s want return punters so they can keep giving the Medicare machine a good thrashing.

Please study this typical Senior Medical Exchange with our Senior Euphemism Translator to guide you through:

Doctor: And how is your alcohol consumption going? = *You look like W.C. Fields.*

Senior: Well, I drink socially now and again. = *I am drunk now and I will be again soon.*

Doctor: How many drinks would you say you have on an average night? = *If you could still speak coherently on an average night. Seriously, Rudolph's nose does not glow as bright as yours. If I lit a match right now my stethoscope would melt.*

Senior: Ah… *(pause for pretend thought)* probably about three or four. = *I fall asleep after my third bottle of wine.*

Doctor: Well, you might want to think about taking it a little easier over the next month. = *Ray Milland's hands shook less in* The Lost Weekend. *So did Kate Hepburn in her last two decades.*

Senior: *(cheerful)* I'll do that. = *I will think about it. I will also think about opening the batting for Australia. The latter is more likely.*

'Check-up' dispensed with, we can then renew our prescriptions and begone.

If Seniors are *actually* sick, rather than just pill shopping, the following G.P. Translator should be memorised:

Doctor: I think this might be a matter for a specialist = *I have no idea what is wrong with you.*

Doctor: There has been a lot of this going around = *I have no idea what is wrong with most of my patients.*

Doctor: I'd like to run some further tests = *I still have no idea what is wrong with you.*

Doctor: Do you have any allergies? = *Is your skin always this dreadful?*

Doctor: I think your sedentary lifestyle is having an adverse effect = *You are fat.*

Doctor: We might just have a look at your blood pressure = *Like Brando fat towards the end. I am surprised you could fit through the door.*

Many G.P.s become informal Specialists themselves, i.e.:

The Mole People: These are G.P.s who become increasingly obsessed with having every single mole, bump, or 'dark circular pattern' cut off your body because they are '*just a bit concerned*'. It's no good pointing out that the dark circular pattern in question is your left nipple, once the Mole People have their scalpels set on you, you will be sliced and diced until they are happy, which is never, as at best they are '*slightly* concerned', especially about that dot on your right pinkie.

Some Doctors become so devoted to the cause that in their spare time they go through old copies of *The Wind in the Willows* with scissors and carefully cut out every time the word Mole is mentioned. (Makes it a better book, actually Ratty and Toad are the stars of the show. Apart from '*Hang Spring Cleaning!*' Moley never says anything memorable or helpful and generally gets in the way. By the way, Ratty, that spot on your right wrist, is that new? Mmm. I think we'd better book you in for next Wednesday 10 am. I'm *just a bit concerned*.)

House Calls: The process of the Doctor deciding what to call his Beach Houses after cutting off all those suckers' moles.

Chiropractors: Chiropractors are frowned upon by many Doctors, probably because these Doctors have sore backs and are grumpy. You'd be grumpy too if you spent seven years at Medical School only to see some back cracker horn in on your turf and earn easy dough from treating patients like play-dough and giving them a few whacks about the back and neck (which is secretly what Doctors would like to do to many Senior Patients who waffle on with '*what's new*' for fifteen minutes before coughing up their symptoms).

Physio: Like massage parlours without the fun bits. After your 'Physio Session', you will nod at various stretches shown to you on pieces of paper which you promise you will do at home. Seniors do many things at home – mainly napping and gardening – but no Senior in history has ever followed instructions from a Physio. If the Physio said '*Go home, make a martini and watch Some Like it Hot*' we might consider it, but as yet this contingency has not arisen.

Holistic Healers: Oh dear. We know Doctors can be patronising but there is no need for Seniors to fly straight into Fairy Land and have mystical herbs with healing properties blown at you by some hipster hippy at surprisingly high prices. (To be fair, they were probably price marked when Healer was high.) Didn't we go through this before in the '60s on communes, except then the drugs actually worked and the music was better?

Half of their 'treatments' seemed to be cribbed from a chapter of *The Magic Faraway Tree* in the first place. Well, we can't stop you wasting your money, the purchase of this book proves that already, but do not come crying to us if you can't get the lavender smell out of your bedroom pillows because of some alleged 'aura daubings'.

Homeopaths: Holistic Healers who are well dressed and have actual office space, instead of a bit of a garden divided by wind chimes.

Christian Science: The oxymoron is the giveaway, isn't it? Strictly speaking, this is not medical treatment, it is not doing anything deliberately, which is eerily similar to what you are doing as you sit in the waiting room of the bloody Medical Centre for 55 minutes. So who is the smart one here, really? Doris Day was a Christian Scientist, looked fab, made it to 97 and could still belt out *'Sentimental Journey'* and *'The Deadwood Stage'* at a moment's notice. Makes you think.

Senior Moments in Hospital

Being Seniors, we sometimes have to visit the Real Doctors at the hospital. This can often be a frightening experience and we advise all Seniors to imagine that the Doctors are speaking in the voice of Cary Grant, which will make their medical advice more reassuring. For instance, if Cary Grant said *'I'd like to keep you overnight for observation'*, this would be a flattering thing to hear. Obviously, the voice doesn't have to be Cary Grant, you can imagine Mae West, Diana Rigg or Groucho Marx; these decisions must be made on a Senior by Senior Basis.

The most important thing to remember for the Senior in Hospital is never be rude to a Nurse. These people watch *One*

Flew Over the Cuckoo's Nest as an instructional video and are not to be trifled with, especially when you would quite like some trifle for dessert please, Nurse, instead of the sub-standard 'tiramisu'.

The not too terribly well hidden secret of hospitals is that you almost *never* see a Doctor anywhere near them; they are run from pillar to post by the Nurses, who also do all the injecting, strapping, feeding and washing. (*Well, if you had just worn a bib as requested while eating your trifle, these steps would not have been necessary.*)

Hospital Visitors: Far more painful than any treatment you receive in the Hospital itself. After your visitors observe the view from the window, tell you how much their parking cost and ask the seemingly obvious question 'So, how are you?' (*Here is a clue, Genius, I am in a hospital*), the awkward silence will then begin. It is very hard to make faltering conversation with someone who is already wondering whether their 45-minute parking ticket will be enough. Do not put up with it. Just tell them that your sponge bath is about begin and have them begone.

CHAPTER 5

Senior Moments in Sports and Leisure

As a Senior you often have time on your hands. As we have been told since childhood, the Devil makes work for idle hands. (This work was never specified, but it could well be wrapping all delivered newspapers in *endless* rolls of thin plastic to drive you *insane* every morning. It is impossible to find the key edge unless you have a jeweller's loop, and even then it never unravels evenly, turning you into a pathetic breakfast version of The Incredible Hulk as you try to rip the now bulked-up remnants off. Once the plastic wrap is off, it then leaves the papers permanently semi-rolled up even when you try to flatten out a corner using the toast plate. Well done, Satan's Helpers, our morning is already ruined.)

Seniors are well advised to fill any empty spaces in their day with the following Senior Sports and Leisure Pursuits, paying close attention to the Tips for Old Players outlined below.

Senior Tennis: Tennis is an excellent game for Seniors as it allows you to play with cunning, rather than the vulgar athleticism of the young. Yes, frantic dashes to return a Lob are out, but your Drop Dead Volley Shot still works in a Doubles Match. Stick to the volleying and leave the lobs alone or you will be the one who drops dead.

When playing singles, the wily Senior will stand on the baseline as much as possible, allowing maximum use of Senior Calling, i.e.:

Another brilliant return from a younger player eludes you

You: Out!
Younger Player: Really? That looked good to me.
You: *(with umbrage at 50% levels)* I am standing *right* on the baseline.
Younger Player: Right. Sorry.

You give a Noblesse Oblige nod, and match continues with you gaining the point and the Moral High Ground

Is this cheating? Well, in a technical and linguistic sense, yes; but the Senior is well advised to heed the wise words of Malcolm X when playing tennis: 'By any means necessary'. (Few people know that Mr X was an excellent tennis player, apart from a tendency to run around his backhand.)

Youth is wasted on the young, and so is accurate calling. Younger players have many unfair advantages of their own, such as knees that still work, and no Senior should feel remotely guilty about redressing this biological disparity with the odd judicious dodgy call.

Senior Golf: Golf is a unique sport in that it can be played badly at any age. The eight-year-old who slices badly will, with practice, one day be the 80-year-old who hooks badly. (We are of course referring to hooking only in the Golfing sense here. If you choose to become a Hooker at the age of 80 we shall make no moral judgements and would in fact be fascinated to know how you do. Please drop a line to the publisher, no photos thank you, he is a prudish fellow and we are sick of his constant threats of litigation.)

Golf is a game almost made for Seniors, as it involves nice walks on well-manicured grounds, frequent chances to see woodland life as you attempt to find your bloody ball and a Clubhouse carefully located at the end of the 18ᵗʰ Hole where you can get pleasantly blotto, feeling fully justified after a day's minimal exertion.

Senior Golfing Terms

Tee: What you had too much of before arriving, which will result in a long walk through the rough to find a discreet tree to relieve yourself. For Female Senior Golfers, a longer walk may be required or a more discrete tree if wearing a skirt.

Par: The man who shattered your confidence at a young age. He has been dead for over 40 years and you can still hear him muttering with disapproval at your irregular grip.

Pro: The handsome young man at the shop who will smilingly tell you that the course is full. If you slip him $20, he will find that *'you may be able to jump on at the seventh'*. If you slip him $200, you may find out he is the *other* type of Pro, but you still won't be able to get on until the seventh as there is a Corporate Day. (It always seems to be a Corporate Day. Do these Corporations even have offices anymore? It seems they spend their entire time Paint-Balling, going on Wilderness Bonding Exercises [not advisable if a Bottlebrush is part of said Wilderness] or delaying Senior Golf. We shall speak to Dow Jones and see what he can do.)

Birdie: The reason your Senior Wife is glaring at you. She is a bartender, there is *no need* to chat to her for that long, you old goat. (*Still thinks he's Cary Grant, pathetic. Ulysses Grant more like.*)

Whippy Shaft: The reason there is really no point even making a play for the Birdie at your age.

Mashie Niblick: Having a nibble while you watch M*A*S*H in the clubhouse because it's raining. Let's hope it's a Trapper John-era episode.

Sand Trap: Betting your Beach House that you can clear the Water Hazard with just a 7-iron. You can't. Luckily the Beach House is in your wife's name and the fellow you made the bet with is even drunker than you and has already fallen into the Water Hazard.

Bogey: He was married to Lauren Bacall. Employed Sam as piano player, and found Maltese Falcon too.

Double-Bogey: They are showing *Key Largo* and *The Treasure of the Sierra Madre* tonight.

Colonel Bogey: A whistling song that informed us that Hitler has only got one ball. He must have been a scratch golfer; we usually lose at least two per round.

Mulligan: A chance to have another bash and forget the fact that you just royally stuffed up your first attempt. Also known as a 'Second Marriage'.

Once the game is over, Experienced Senior Golfers will lose no time in taking up a balcony position *over* the 18th. It is there, beer in hand, that Seniors can gaze magisterially at the poor sods hacking their way *up* the 18th. If the wind is blowing the right way, as they make their last botched club stroke to approach the green, the players will be able to hear your disapproving *'Tch'*.

They shall then turn to see you, as Solemn Golfing Senior, shaking your head, more in sorrow than in anger, as you clearly know the *shot that should have been*. The fact that *you* just shot 136 will never be known to them, as you can finish your hooch and be driving smugly home before they have even finished putting.

Lawn Bowls: Bowls is an ancient sport usually played by ancient people such as yourself. Yes, it is *the* cliché Senior Sport, but there is a good reason for that: it is *tremendous* fun and not just when you give up on the jack completely and smash your opponent's secondary bowl into the ditch for kicks. (If Senior Bowlers are honest, they will admit this is 50% of the reason they play.) The truly extraordinary thing about Lawn Bowls is that the people who play it are invariably *cheerful*.

Most Senior Sports are strewn with players who could give John McEnroe a run for his money in a temper-tantrum contest. Golf is a particular offender; it is a rare Senior Golfer indeed who has a complete set of irons in their bag, usually at least two have been thrown into a watery grave after one yip too many on the back nine. But Senior Bowlers are *universally* chipper and relaxed. We think it may be the uniforms. (Or the fact that they usually have a stealthy drink during match play.)

If we all dressed in white, wore a sensible sun hat and sipped on an occasional Pimm's when nobody was looking, the world would be a better place. (Especially for the Pimm's people, they *owned* the 1950's, barely see them out anymore. The Jerry Lee Lewis of gins.)

Bridge: Bridge is poker for Seniors who don't like to lose money but still enjoy arguing with their spouse once a week about whether they *should* have bid six or seven in front of another couple who are still not speaking after prematurely pre-empting to the third level. Bridge players take the byzantine rules and tactics of their game very seriously indeed, far more seriously than most Engineers do when they build actual bridges.

It has always been thus, in fact in the 1950's, Bridge caused more divorces than adultery. If you understated the value of a singleton you could very shortly find yourself a singleton *and* lose custody if you got a Bridge Sympathetic Judge. To this day most post-dinner Bridge games end in bitter puns about 'dummies' and with at least one scene: 'Well, I *thought* I had Five Hearts, but now I know you have *none*, Jerry!' (*Exeunt in tears.*)

As such, Seniors should try to remember it is only a game, although how *anyone* could play the King of Spades and *miss* such an *obvious* Slam is *beyond me*, Daphne!

Omar Sharif was very good at Bridge, which is something all Bridge players will tell you within five minutes of meeting them. He was also very good in *Lawrence of Arabia*, which featured no Bridge whatsoever, unlike David Lean's other masterpiece, *Bridge on the River Kwai*, where Alec Guinness led the nine of spades from dummy and ran it, before realising his ghastly mistake and falling on the detonator. This is not even in the top five over-reactions we have seen from Senior Bridge Players. Lighten up, please.

Senior Cricket: Even Test cricketers know they should hang it up around the age of 40, but Senior Cricketers are determined fellows and can keep going right into their 70's, or even longer if the other players agree to use their coffin as the stumps.

The reason they cannot give it up is because they are Cricket Tragics; the tragic bit being they still think they can get away with playing a Leg Glance at their age. Sadder still are the bowlers who insist on declaring themselves 'Medium-Pacers', which is only remotely true if they are referring to the setting level of their pacemakers.

Cricket is known as the 'Gentleman's Game' by gentlemen who have never played cricket. The language levelled at the average Senior Batsman when he walks out by the Slips Cauldron alone would get them convicted at The Hague.

According to the *'spirit of cricket'*, if a Senior Batsman gently snicks a ball to the keeper, he should walk if the Umpire does not hear it and calls him 'Not Out'. According the *'reality of cricket'*, even if the ball thunks off his bat louder than the average concert by The Who, a Senior Batsman is about as likely to walk as Christopher Reeve in the final decade of his life. (Yes, we are aware that joke is tasteless; we heard it from the Slips Cauldron.)

Chess: Many Seniors are put off by Chess because a) they don't understand the rules and b) it was that creepy game that Death played in Ingmar Bergman's *The Seventh Seal*. (A most disappointing film, we watched closely but could only see three seals and a porpoise. This was a step up on most Art Films, which pride themselves on having no porpoise whatsoever.)

Chess is game suited to the Senior because it allows for long significant pauses while you stare meaningfully at the board. These pauses can go on for at least five minutes before your opponent realises you are napping and slaps you awake, then forces you to forfeit your Bishop. (Unlike in real life, Bishops are quite useful in Chess and keep a respectful distance from the Pawns even when there is nobody watching.)

If you are a Senior playing Chess against a Younger Player and sense you are in trouble, the following tactic always works: simply move your Knight in any direction and then say *'Checkmate in three, I believe'* in a lordly fashion. Extend your hand patronisingly for the victory shake and you should be out the door before they even realise that you *should not trust anyone over 60*.

One interesting thing about Chess is that many Grand Masters go completely off their nut, like Bobby Fischer, who believed that Boris Spassky was tapping his phone and his cornflakes. One of these things may well have been true, but when Fischer kept going on and on about the missing seals in Ingmar Bergman movies they knew he had lost it.

Backgammon: Give up and play checkers, you know you have no idea what you are doing.

CHAPTER 6

Senior Moments from the 20ᵗʰ Century

SENIORS WILL HOPEFULLY HAVE A VAGUE RECOLLECTION OF these selected historic events, either from real life or Cinesound Newsreels. Both often involved a packet of Jaffas and wondering if it was *time to make a move*. Usually you played it safe and stuck to the Jaffas, which would also stick to you if you sat on them after making an unsuccessful move.

1938: The Munich Agreement: Neville Chamberlain and his umbrella both seemed thrilled with this agreement when they got off that small plane and waved a piece of white paper in the air, but as the agreement was '*Let's Trust Mr Hitler To Do The Right Thing*' it turned out to be one of the worst agreements made in the history of the planet, even narrowly beating the agreement to commission the solo album *Ringo's Rotogravure*.

There were many roll-on effects from the Munich Agreement, including obviously tanks rolling over Poland within a year, but one little noted is the disappearance of the name Neville. Neville Wran did his best to get it going again, but there were no further takers.

1951: Douglas MacArthur Says 'I shall return!': He said this quite a lot, actually, especially when shopping for sweaters that were declared 'pre-shrunk' in Department Stores. An odd fellow, whether it was WW2 or Korea, MacArthur liked to hop out of ships before they had hit the beach so he could be photographed manfully striding ashore. Yes, it looked cool, but his socks were not pre-shrunk and resulted in many years of exposed ankle whenever he crossed his legs wearing long trousers.

This may not sound like a big deal today, but the very thought of exposed ankle or, God help you, shin, haunted all Senior Men in the 1950's. If you ever watch an old episode of *Leave it to Beaver*, you will notice that Ward Cleaver always carefully hitches his pants and enacts an elegant two-handed pinch gesture on his trouser fronts before he sits down to avoid ankle showage. What happened to this move and this fear? We suggest Seniors bring both back as soon as possible.

Anyway, MacArthur got fired mid-Korean War by President Truman for being too big for his boots. MacArthur tried to argue that was because his socks were pre-shrunk but Harry would not listen. In his famous valedictory speech, MacArthur declared '*Old soldiers never die, they just fade away*'. This was another whopper, he died in 1964. He *may* return, but it's been over 50 years and he is taking his sweet time.

1957: Sputnik is Launched: This was the first satellite to be launched into space. Before then, Satellite Interviews were a pointless affair, as the Satellite was mostly metal and would rarely say anything, not even 'I'm sorry, I can't do that, Hal'. This was the start of the Space Race, which the Russians surprisingly looked like winning at this point.

They launched Yuri Gagarin into space (in a rocket, not a slingshot, although that option was seriously considered before the Russians realised the Warner Bros. shorts were animated) and also a dog named Belka, either as company for Yuri or to help run the satellite. We don't know if Belka is still personally running the show, but if she is, our Foxtel Dish has been acting up lately; if she could lend a paw and check on it from her end we would be most grateful.

1960: The Berlin Wall is Built: A tragedy but also remarkable in that it was the only time in the past 100 years that a construction project was finished ahead of schedule, let alone overnight. We still don't know how the Reds got council approval so quickly; it usually takes us eight months to get even a mailbox provisionally considered for stage one consultation.

1962: The Cuban Missile Crisis: A Nuclear Holocaust loomed for 13 days until it turned out the missiles were not Cuban at all, but belonged to Russia. Silly old Khrushchev, one would have thought he would have remembered this from the start. Funny chap; used to take his shoe off and bang it on the table when he got angry. Luckily, the shoes were made in Russia and would disintegrate on contact with any hard surface, thus leaving the table unscuffed, but still, bad manners. We will not mention what President Kennedy used to bang on the table, but suffice it to say he would have done very, very poorly in the 'Me Too' era.

1963: JFK Assassinated: Where were you when Kennedy was shot? Every Senior can answer this question. If your answer is 'standing on the grassy knoll with my umbrella gun' then we advise you to keep this to yourself. Lee Harvey Oswald claimed that he was a Patsy, but the only Patsy proven to be in the area at the time was Patsy Cline, who did a wonderful version of '*Crazy*' but other than that, was not much help to the FBI.

Oswald himself was shot dead by Jack Ruby, a local nightclub owner who had a sideline in starting bizarre conspiracy theories, which we must admit he pulled off pretty well on this occasion.

Seriously, Seniors, do not go down this rabbit hole: you will never come out. The only suspect we have ruled out so far is JFK.

1964: The British Invasion: It was not a literal invasion, but it did do quite a bit of damage to AM radio. It started with The Beatles who were undoubtedly a good thing, as were The Stones and The Who. The invasion got a little icky though with Freddie and the Dreamers and Gerry and the Pacemakers, and by the time bloody Herman's Hermits turned up you could not escape from a British accent singing either a long ballad or music hall ditty every time you fired up the wireless. Even Elvis had to spend the entire decade making rotten movies before he was allowed back on the radio with '*Suspicious Minds*'.

1966: 'All the Way With LBJ': Prime Minister Harold Holt declared this to be Australia's confusing policy regarding the Vietnam War. As Seniors will recall, 'LBJ' was only third base, 'all the way' was saved for marriage. It was an interesting insight into the Holt marriage, and we did not hear a major politician refer to LBJ again publicly until Bill Clinton and Monica.

1969: The Moon Landing: It may have been one small step for man, but it was one *very* long wait if you were actually watching it on TV. We do not know if Neil was trying to sober up Buzz in the Lunar Capsule, but it took a suspiciously long time for those lads to get out and go for a very, very slow walk. To be honest, it *was* awesome and historic but ever so slightly dull. Subsequent Astronauts brought along Golf Clubs and Dune Buggies to liven things up a bit, but it didn't really help.

The fact that the Moon Landings took far too long and were rather boring for the average audience member led to much speculation that they were shot by Stanley Kubrick. We doubt this, but we know for a fact Kubrick did *not* shoot JFK as he would have demanded over 50 takes, by which time Lee Harvey Oswald would have turned the gun on Stanley.

1974: Crankie Frankie Gets Stuck in Australia: This was a fun one. Frank Sinatra found himself landlocked by the Unions after getting stuck *into* Australia. During a concert in Melbourne, Mr Sinatra paused in between Cole Porter classics to declare that all Australian female journalists were 'buck-and-a-half hookers'. This was clearly defamatory as most of them charged a lot more than that and in any case this was the Seventies, when it was a point of pride for all feminists who had read Erica Jong to give it away for nothing.

Francis Albert went on to describe all Australian *male* journalists as 'pimps', which got the Transport Workers Union on his back as this obviously caused a demarcation dispute. Eventually, Bob Hawke was called in to negotiate and drink Frank under the table; whereupon both Bob and an agreement were struck. Bob granted approval to let Mr Sinatra's plane leave the country as long as he never attempted to cover *'Mrs Robinson'* ever again.

1972–74: Watergate: The Watergate Scandal was incredibly complicated and not even Robert Redford and Dustin Hoffman understood the plot entirely. Apparently G. Gordon Liddy, determined to find out what the first G. stood for, tried to burgle the Democrat National Committee Headquarters at the Watergate Building. It was easy to get in as the gate was made of water, which was decorative and soothing but terrible for National Security.

Also terrible for National Security were Ehrlichman and Haldeman, who were *All the President's Men*, even though there were only two of them and strictly speaking they should have been *Both The President's Men*. Or Mans.

Angered at such third-rate grammar, President Nixon held a Press Conference to announce that '*I am not a crook*' and to prove it also announced that he had taped everybody's conversations in the Oval Office, as honest people do. This caused something of a panic, especially to the President when he listened back to the tapes and realised that he *was* in fact a crook.

Luckily, the President's secretary, an obliging woman named Rose Mary Woods, after many hours of careful effort, accidentally erased the most damaging 18 minutes of the tapes and a relieved Nixon declared '*I am not a quitter*' before quitting immediately.

Nixon was pardoned by his successor, Gerald Ford, and went off to sulk at San Clemente and wait for David Frost to interview him for over 8 hours, which all agreed was punishment enough.

1975: Gough Gets the Sack: Despite being elected Prime Minister in a process then known as democracy, Mr Whitlam found himself removed because he could not guarantee supply. This has happened to many drug dealers but to only one Australian Prime Minister so far. A normal man would be depressed at this stroke of ill fortune, but Gough found it a golden opportunity to release his famous witticism: '*Well may we say God Save the Queen, because nothing can save Freddy Mercury's Solo Career*'.

Although he was right, Mr Whitlam was defeated by a record margin at the next two elections, despite carefully explaining to the electorate how much cleverer he was than them.

In his later years, Whitlam patented his invention 'Gough Syrup', a strawberry-tasting liquid that would make you incredibly arrogant about your time in office if you had two teaspoons a day. It had a limited market, but several Former PMs swear by it (and because of it).

1979: Maggie Becomes PM: Margaret Thatcher became the first woman to be the Prime Minister of England, with the possible exception of Lord Salisbury, though nothing could be proved. Despite being known as 'The Iron Lady' she never starred in a single Marvel movie, let alone getting a whole franchise like Robert Downey Jr.

After a record four terms of unpopularity, Thatcher was sacked after the disastrous Pole Tax, which did not work as Poles had no money and just helped Telephone Wires be strung appropriately. Thatcher thought seriously about taxing the North Pole as she believed, quote 'that fat bastard Santa must be loaded', but by then it was too late and John Major had already bored himself into office.

A controversial figure at the best of times, Maggie terrified the opposition, her own cabinet and especially Denis, her long-suffering husband who spent most of his time hiding in No. 10 Downing Street hoping that he would blend in with the furniture. He succeeded in this task all too well, leading to his being forgotten on departure and being used as an Ottoman for several years by John Major.

1983: Australia Wins the America's Cup: For 130 years, Australian millionaires and then billionaires wondered why the General Public took little interest in a group of incredibly rich guys racing yachts. Although many Australians drank schooners, most of them could not give a stuff about racing them, sticking to tinnies for both drinking and fishing purposes.

All of this changed in 1983, thanks to a colourful billionaire named Alan Bond. Seniors will recall that Bond was not actually colourful, he was mildly tanned at the best of times, but 'colourful' is a euphemism used by Australian journalists to mean 'crook but we can't prove it yet/they have already paid off the cops'.

In a race to acquire respectability before he went to prison, Bond recruited a taciturn Skipper named John Bertrand. (The actual Skipper from *Gilligan's Island*, Alan Hale Jr, was unavailable, being stuck on an island somewhere with the S.S. *Minnow* and the Harlem Globetrotters at the time for a reunion movie.)

An enigmatic genius named Ben Lexcen designed his famous 'winged keel', a device that many argued was illegal. Being illegal never worried Bondy however, and in 1983 *Australia II* won the America's Cup, narrowly beating *Rocky III* and *Henry IV*. A delighted Australia got drunk, urged on by Bob Hawke, who told Frank Sinatra he was a bum, just to rub it in. Sadly, the Americans won their Cup back the next time and Australia went back to using the Mug With The Small Chip In It that was still perfectly fine, but not quite the same.

1986: Malcolm Fraser Gets Caught in Memphis with No Trousers: We still can't believe this actually happened. Malcolm Fraser, the previously dignified former Prime Minister of Australia, turned up at reception in a third-rate Memphis Hotel without any trousers and asked the nice lady at reception if she might redress this state of undress.

Long rumoured to be a Pants Man, it was thus doubly ironic that Mal found himself unaccountably pants-free at the precise moment an Australian journalist walked into the reception and had his jaw permanently dropped in astonishment. Mr Fraser promptly declared himself to have been drugged and could therefore not remember anything, starting presumably with his pants.

Mr Fraser had also lost his Rolex, his wallet, his passport, his dignity and his credibility, but rather than bother the Memphis Police with these trifles, he decided to hotfoot it back to Oz and stay schtum. *What* Malcolm was doing in Memphis, *why* he was staying in a very seedy Hotel called *The Admiral Benbow* and *what happened to his trousers* were three lingering mysteries that Tammy brought up during every argument for the rest of the poor man's life.

We can but speculate, but will note that it was amazing what you could get away with before Mobile Phones, the Internet and Twitter ruined all the fun.

CHAPTER 7

Senior Moments at Funerals

Tips for Non-Beginners

We shall say this for funerals: they have maintained their form, unlike the hippy-dippy pagan travesties that constitute most 'weddings', funerals still take place in a church with all the men wearing suits and ties. (Including the corpse if it's a man or, heaven forbid, Diane Keaton, one day soon.)

Attending funerals is one of the more depressing aspects of being a Senior. Of course, it could be worse, you could be the star of the show. Then again, if you were the corpse at least you wouldn't have to listen to the 30-ish Minister fumbling about for suitable vagaries while pretending they knew or at least remembered the dearly departed. ('I wonder how many of us knew the *real* Deidre?' is always the giveaway. Of course we knew the real Deidre, that's why we are here, chump. Are you suggesting Deidre had a double, like Monty in WW2? No, you just haven't got the foggiest who she is. Man up, read *Psalm 23* and get on with it.)

When to Arrive: Never come early to a funeral, you will invariably have to make small talk with a maiden aunt whose name you have forgotten and find yourself lost in a game of twenty questions to figure out whether they are on your mother's or your father's side. Sometimes they are neither and turn out to be the obligatory maiden aunt who attends all funerals wearing pearls and a slightly too big hat.

Savvy Seniors will leave their entry late, knowing that it is always dramatic to enter just before the service begins. The more daring male Senior will walk straight to the front pew and give a knowing nod to the Widow along with a slightly too fond kiss before they take their seat. This helps to create an air of mystery and gives the congregants something to think about other than what *on earth* happened to traditional stained-glass windows?

Did they forget how to do it in 1966 because the glass makers were all on acid or something? Is that supposed to be a dove or an angel with a strange nose, etc.?

Eulogy Euphemisms For Seniors

In the days of yore only one person delivered the eulogy, which usually meant you stood a good chance of getting out of the chapel for Morning Tea. Nowadays, the Funeral Eulogy often degenerates into a sort of delayed 21st party for the deceased, with a conga line of acquaintances and distant relatives popping up each to tell a five-minute 'anecdote' which invariably revolves around *them* with a token appearance by the dearly departed.

One would have thought the fact that the word 'Eulogy' is *singular* would have been enough to prevent this practice, but apparently not. Seriously, we have been to funerals where the Minister has asked if anybody *would like to come up and say a few words*! Is this an open mike night? Get on with it.

If you are asked to deliver *the* Eulogy, please observe the following traditional euphemisms:

'**They did not suffer fools gladly**' = incredibly rude and bad tempered. (And by the way, who does suffer fools gladly? Con men presumably as they bilk the fools of their life savings while pretending to change them to a cheaper electricity plan.)

'**They were the life of the party**' = a drunk.

'**A real character**' = a drunk *or* insane, often both if the deceased is Irish. (Irish readers, don't get upset, the author of this book is Irish and three sheets to the wind right now. This is of course a joke: Irish people don't write, they are too drunk to type.)

'**A true gentleman**' = forgot to ask you to pay back the money he lent you.

'**A true lady**' = always slapped your face when you made a pass.

'**They lived life to the full**' = multiple affairs.

'**I still can't believe that they are dead**' = suspect Trophy Wife couldn't wait for inheritance. Autopsy pending.

'**Of staunch/firm views**' = made Marshal Tito look left wing.

'**They loved life**' = refused to sign the euthanasia forms despite best efforts of children.

'**They did not go gently into that good night**' = slapped a Nurse/swore at Doctor.

'**They broke the mould when they made him**' = he was not exactly a rival to Tyrone Power in the looks department.

And of course we cannot forget these Senior Perennials:

'**Never married**' = homosexual.

'**A confirmed bachelor**' = homosexual.

'**He and his wife never had an argument in 50 years of wedded bliss**' = homosexual.

Seniors have sat through innumerable eulogies. If you are about to give a eulogy and we have to listen, PLEASE AVOID THE FOLLOWING CLICHES:

'**I suppose God needed an extra angel in heaven.**' No, he doesn't, the place is chock-a-block with them. Plus, he's God, do you really think he couldn't wait for a chit-chat with your Aunt Ethel? Jane Austen, Shakespeare and Jimi Hendrix are already up there, I think God is doing fine on the entertainment front.

'**Taken from us.**' Aunt Ethel was 87! Makes God seem like he's a hitman in *The Day of the Jackal* or something. She wasn't 'taken from us', she finally left, like a Danish au pair who got the hint the 55th time your wife glared at her when she wore that low-cut top. My God, she was a peach. Two peaches actually, hence the glares.

'**In a way, I feel they are with us today.**' They are, they are in the pine box up the front, pay attention nitwit.

'**Too beautiful for this world.**' Really? Audrey Hepburn was quite a stunner and the world managed to put up with her for seven decades. Sophia Loren is still going! Elle Macpherson still healthy, too. Think of another reason they carked it.

'**They are probably looking down on us right now and smiling.**' No, once again they are in the box at the front hopefully with the lid closed. If they are smiling, it would be due to an oddity of rigor mortis or an embalmer with a sick sense of humour. Certainly nothing to do with your eulogy, which has hardly been a thigh slapper.

Funeral Songs

Hymns were written for a reason, you know. Many of them have music by Bach who was the Adele of his day. Please think twice, then three times, then think 'no', before deciding to play a 'special favourite of the deceased'. We like '*The Piano Man*' too and we would rather not get depressed the next time we hear it thinking about your bloody funeral.

(Actually, '*The Piano Man*' is quite a depressing song anyway. Why is Davy still in the Navy if he hates it so much? They stopped having Press Gangs in the 18th century. There is no need to be in it 'for life', Davy. As for Paul the 'Real Estate Novelist', give it up, Paul, how many good novels do you know about real estate? Okay, *Brideshead Revisited*, but what else?)

The following pop songs are acceptable, if you must, for a Senior Funeral:

'**My Way**' **by Frank Sinatra.** You can always use a little Frank at a funeral to cheer you up. Plus, it's a very good rebuttal song to most eulogies. Most people did not actually do it 'their way', including Frank who did it Ava Gardner's way before she gave him the flick for some bullfighter. Anyway, good rousing stuff which will get us through to the first Scotch at the Wake.

'**We'll Meet Again**' **by Vera Lynn.** Makes everybody seem like they were a WW2 Flying Ace. In fact, you needed a sick bag every time an Ansett plane started to taxi, but still. Plus, we admire the ghoulish undertone of this selection: 'We *will* meet again, don't know where and hopefully *not* when.'

'In the Mood' by Glenn Miller. Peter Sellers used this one as he was being cremated, still makes us laugh.

Traditional Parlour Game to Play At Funerals: Who's Next?

Arguably tasteless and undeniably morbid, the Bored Senior can, and – be honest – invariably does, entertain themselves during the hymns by playing the mental game of '*Who's Next?*' Who shall it be? Where shall the fickle finger of fate poke next? Cousin Susan? *(Her make-up thicker than usual, why?)* Uncle Bertie? *(His hand quavering even when clutching that stick. Curious.)* Makes you feel like a psychic Poirot.

Do not on any account lay money on the thing; you will be amazed at how many wavering spinsters in their mid-nineties outlast twenty-something great-nephews brazenly checking their mobiles during the service. (By the by, if you do wager, a good stealth bet is always 'the Minister', you can get excellent odds and they have a surprisingly high death rate. Makes you wonder if God thinks they're doing a terribly good job, doesn't it?)

The After-Funeral

'*Are you coming round?*' Usually something screamed at you by Burgess Meredith in a boxing ring, it is the guilt-ridden *sotto voce* chorus question that rings out from any relative of the deceased. One would think you have already scored points by actually turning up for the funeral. But no, all credits will be eliminated unless you appear to devour crust-free salmon paste finger sandwiches at a 'gathering'. Like the world's most depressing after party, but with extremely nice china. Grin and bear it or they won't turn up to yours.

Now, there is an entirely different after-funeral known as:

The Wake

You have to hand it to the Irish (seriously, give it to them now or they will steal it). They never lose any opportunity to get rolling drunk, and the death of a loved one is not an exception, it is a rule. If you have never been to an Irish wake, imagine a New Orleans jazz procession meets a nightclub brawl held at a garden party and you get some idea. Masses of people drunk, yelling, laughing and weeping at the same time – and that's just the children.

Seriously, I once attended a wake for a Great Uncle, only to have a distant Senior Cousin brilliantly re-enact the infamous butter scene from *Last Tango in Paris* using only a sausage roll as Marlon Brando, a whisky bottle, a French accent and a triumph of imagination; all of this with my just-widowed Great Aunt looking on in wonder and admiration. When I actually saw the film in question, it was a let-down, he was that good. That was only the 4th strangest thing that happened at that Wake.

If you as a Senior ever get the chance to go to a Wake, jump on it: the Irish may have no idea how to live happily but they sure as hell know how to die with a bang. Yes Virginia, there *is* such a thing as a happy Irishman; he is at a Wake.

Ashes to Ashes

If you are a Senior who chooses to be cremated, the chance then comes for a final bit of fun and inconvenience for your family: where to place the ashes?

Don't just say 'the sea' or 'the Adelaide Oval'. Try to make it something intriguingly specific such as 'To be thrown upon the resting place of Mamie Van Doren, at dusk, as the poem "*The Highwayman*" is read, preferably by a light tenor. Those in attendance are respectfully requested to wear Venetian masks and each bring a lemur.' The more questions it leaves the better.

Senior Headstones

Do not be bashful when it comes to choosing an inscription. Your name, dates and '*Beloved Husband and Father*' are just not going to cut it in the attention stakes for those idly strolling through the graveyard in years hence. An inscription does not have to be long to gain interest: '*I Blame Marjorie*' will do the job.

A touch of verse is always nice, i.e. '*Ashes to Ashes/Dust to Dust/ Susan Wouldn't But Maggie Must*'. True Crime is perennially popular; if you inscribe '*The So-Called Rushcutter Strangler (Acquitted)*' on your tombstone, you are bound to get foot traffic and Instagram pics in the future.

CHAPTER 8

Senior Moments: Missing in Action

As a Senior you will have noticed that among the many ways Modern Life is disappointing is the disappearance of the following familiar staples of yesteryear. What happened to them? (If you spot any of them in the wild, drop us a line.)

Women Called 'Peg': Used to be everywhere, now vanished. Laundry Pegs are the sole reminder that they used to flourish amongst us. (Come to think of it, Pirates used to have Peg-Legs too but they don't anymore. Is it a co-incidence?)

Mr Manners: You remember, you used to leave a biscuit on a plate for him. Nowadays it seems people only leave a biscuit alone because they've *gone paleo* and are looking for an excuse to tell you about it at great length. (Apparently these loons think the secret of perfect health is to eat like a caveman. The fact that none of the cavemen lived past 33 doesn't seem to worry them.)

Movies With An Intermission: In the old days when any flick went for a second longer than two hours you used to get an intermission. With a David Lean film you got at least two, including a packed lunch and a cot if you were trying to make it through *Doctor Zhivago*. Today moviemakers must think we all have the bladder control of Harry Houdini; the films all go for three hours and every drink you can buy at the Candy Bar is at least two litres. Sadists. Give us a break, Hollywood, literally.

Chest Expanders: At one time this was the sole piece of exercise equipment kept in any home. Now people have entire gymnasiums in their spare room with machinery that would dazzle a Russian Cosmonaut but the chest expander has mysteriously gone AWOL. We are not conspiracy buffs, but we note that right after all the chest expanders disappeared, men's stomachs started expanding. You do the math.

Hotel Rooms With Keys: No, not 'key cards', actual metal keys that actually worked. You used to get them back in the days when the hotel didn't assume every guest was a cat burglar. Now it is pot luck whether your 'key card' will even let you have the honour of using the lift, let alone open the door to your own room without shoving it in and out of a slot 17 times to master the secret split-second timing that will finally get that little bloody red light to go green and let you in. Hard enough when sober, if you've had a couple of drinks you may as well give up and sleep in the corridor.

Thin Moustaches: Ronald Colman had one, David Niven did too. Now every man with a moustache looks like they are trying to win a Henry Lawson Lookalike Competition.

The Speaking Clock: It used to be so reassuring to ring a number and listen to a baritone filled with certainty tell you what the time would be at the third stroke. Nowadays you will have three strokes before you get through to anyone on the telephone, and nobody has a baritone anymore, even the opera stars are all tenors. If Paul Robeson was still alive he would make a fortune (which he would have to give away because he was a pinko, that's what my aunt used to mutter every time *Sanders of the River* came on the television).

People Who Could Recite Verse: Which they would do at the drop of a hat or three drops of any form of liquor. *The Road to Mandalay*, *The Rubaiyat of Omar Khayyam*, bits of Byron, tons of Tennyson you had been forced to learn at school, or – for those modishly daring – something from the 20th century: a dash of Dylan Thomas or Betjeman. Uncle Albert would not leave a dinner party without reciting at least three verses of *Miss Joan Hunter Dunne*. Of course, that meant he was not invited to any dinner parties, but this suited everybody. When was the last time you heard anybody recite anything that rhymed apart from '*The Good Ship Venus*' at a Rugby Dinner?

Goon Show Impressions: Like the Goons themselves: long gone, I'm afraid. 30 years ago you would not get through a day without hearing somebody doing a spot-on Eccles or a half-decent Bluebottle, and I'm told on good authority that the Queen Mother herself used to do an excellent Major Bloodnok after she'd had two bottles of bubbly (which was about 10 am by the way). But these days even if you wait for the exact right moment to say 'He's fallen in the water!' all you'll get is puzzled silence and a glare from the lifeguard. Try singing the '*Ying Tong Song*' and they'll lock you up.

Cole's Funny Picture Book: No, it had nothing to with the supermarket. Like the Bible and a copy of *Robinson Crusoe* it was in every Australian home, but unlike the other two you actually read it when you got bored. Okay, it wasn't particularly funny, but the optical illusion tests were fun and that giant whipping machine for boys is still a good idea that I often think about when the little brats are being unruly in adult restaurants. What are they doing in here anyway?

The 'White Slave Trade': What happened to it? Every young lady used to walk about secretly feeling important because at any moment they could be whisked away to some far-flung Harem land where a wicked sheik who looked just like Omar Sharif would do unspeakable things to you. Now there aren't any unspeakable things, people speak about all of them and make instructional videos. Did you see 'Fifty Shades of Grey'? Filthy. I have the Blu-ray.

CHAPTER 9
Senior Moments in Jazz

As Seniors know, before there was 'Rock Music' there was Jazz, music that contained actual melody and was played by musicians who had taken music lessons. Many of the singers could also sing, mostly in key, with the exception of Billie Holiday. She got away with it because of her incredible 'phrasing', which was Billie's term for when the junk kicked in and she sang slightly faster with less slurring.

(We are teasing, we *love* Billie Holiday and imagine we would be quite fond of heroin too, but do not want to end up like Charlie Parker who took so much of the stuff he believed he was a Bird and would only tweet into the saxophone, to the despair of Norman Granz.)

Please enjoy the following Senior Trip Down Memory Lane looking at **Jazz: People, Places and Things**.

Louis Armstrong: The father of Jazz, he caused decades of trouble for DJs who were not sure whether his first name was pronounced '*Lewis*' or '*Louey*'. Unsure of the right way to say it himself, due to all the reefer, in order to save trouble Armstrong was known as '*Satchmo*' and played with either the *Hot Fives* or the *Hot Sevens*, depending on how many musicians were standing near the air conditioning in the studio at the time.

Armstrong himself was *continually* sweating and dabbed theatrically at his forehead at all times with a spotted handkerchief. During some of the faster cornet solos a mop was applied so he wouldn't drown in the middle of *'Potato Head Blues'*.

Satchmo played like an angel but sang like somebody was continually pouring gravel down his throat, which sounded marvellous nonetheless. He was also great in *High Society* with Bing, Crankie Frankie and Grace Kelly, despite the fact that in this otherwise fun film he and Bing sing the *least* jazzy song of all time, ironically called *'That's Jazz'*.

Satchmo had his biggest hit 18 years after he was dead with his rendition of *'What a Wonderful World'*. As Seniors know, the world is *not* wonderful, most of it is rotten when looked at objectively, but Satchmo was so beloved he could make you believe anything for 3 minutes and 10 seconds, which luckily was the exact running time of the song.

Duke Ellington: Not a real Duke, in the same way that Nat King Cole was not of royal blood, although he was a second cousin of Old King Cole, who as Senior Jazz Students will recall, had Fiddlers Three. We cannot recall who was in the Fiddlers Three, one of whom was probably Stéphane Grappelli, as he fiddled on everything except his taxes. (Stéphane's taxes were done by Django Reinhardt, who was a carefree Gypsy but bloody careful when it came to offsetting assets from the previous tax year.)

Anyway, Duke Ellington was great, wrote *'Mood Indigo'*, *'Take The "A" Train'* (catchy as hell, and infuriated the owners of the "B" train who lost many customers to its punchy beat) and of course *'It Don't Mean a Thing (If It Ain't Got That Swing)'*. Using the word 'ain't' was the closest the Duke ever came to being inelegant; he was a snappy dresser, snappy composer and snappy Bandleader, who once slapped Mel Torme when he attempted to sing *'Sophisticated Lady'* in falsetto for a lark.

A genius and a gent, he also scored *Anatomy of a Murder* with Jimmy Stewart. (To be clear, Jimmy just acted in the thing, he couldn't write for toffee, although he was good at pretending to be Glenn Miller.)

Ella Fitzgerald: The possessor of possibly the most pure, beautiful and consistently perfect voice ever heard by man, with Jimmy Durante running a close second, 'Lady Ella' was the undisputed Queen of the Jazz Era.

Pioneering the concept of the album, she had million sellers with *Ella Sings the Cole Porter Song Book*, *Ella Sings the George and Ira Gershwin Song Book* and, to prove a point, *Ella Sings Jerome Kern's Phone Book* – a two-disc set consisting simply of Ella melodically scatting the names and addresses in said volume. (Surprisingly, Old Man River was not listed in the address book, leading to suspicions that Kern had just made him up, although he pointed the finger at Oscar Hammerstein Snr. and Jnr.)

Ella's first smash hit was actually just a nursery rhyme 'A-Tisket, A-Tasket', the not terribly gripping story of a girl who had temporarily misplaced her Yellow Basket. Ella's perfect pipes and her invention of 'scat' turned the thing into a sensation. Do not look up 'scat' on the internet – you will be in for a rude shock – instead, put on *Ella Sings the Rodgers & Hart Song Book* and have a cocktail as you think of how marvellous everything used to be.

Bing Crosby: These days we only hear Der Bingle warbling away at Christmas time, but he did a lot more than sing *'Mele Kalikimaka'* with The Andrews Sisters, although this alone would have been enough to guarantee him immortality.

Crosby was the first of 'The Crooners'; before him, all singers had to yell at the back of the theatre, with Al Jolson practically becoming an air siren in his desire to belt the crowd into submission. Bing figured out that if you just leant forward and breathed softly into the microphone, it would sound super sexy, and indeed it did when he sang 'Temptation' or 'Out of Nowhere'.

After a while he stopped being sexy and became a beloved family man, except by his actual family, who were scared to death of him. Apparently, Bing was a strict disciplinarian who would beat his sons with a belt for practically any transgression, including weekly weight gain or liking Frank Sinatra. True, he would try to soften the punishment by beating the boys rhythmically while singing 'Swinging on a Star', but it still hurt; and swinging on anything was out of the question until their bottoms had at least a night to recover.

Bing was not just a singer, he was also in a bunch of terrific 'Road To' movies with his pal Bob Hope and the gorgeous Dorothy Lamour; was great as a fun priest in Going My Way and won an Academy Award for pulling off the incredibly difficult feat of looking miserable while sleeping with Grace Kelly in The Country Girl.

Bing could sing almost anything with almost everybody, which he proved weeks before his death by duetting with David Bowie in a bizarre but beautiful rendition of 'Little Drummer Boy (Peace on Earth)'. One wonders what they talked about between takes. We only hope Bing did not discover that Mr Bowie named his son Zowie Bowie or Bing's belt would have been off and whacking in a flash, sure as eggs.

The Andrew Sisters: They sang in perfect harmony but that was where the harmony ended. The Andrews Sisters fought so loudly and so long that during WW2 General Eisenhower had to personally ask them to keep it down during D-Day as it was upsetting the men on both sides.

But by God, LaVerne, Maxene and Patty could sing; 'The Boogie Woogie Bugle Boy' still puts a spring in any step, even though everybody *hates* the sound of a bugle as it means being woken up and having an RSM yell at you, or two of the other Andrews Sisters yell at you if you were in the group itself.

The Andrews Sisters also gave all G.I.s the melodic order: '*Don't Sit Under the Apple Tree (With Anyone Else But Me)*'. This was fine with the G.I.s because they just sat under the Lemon Tree instead and made out like crazy. (Not with each other, that was illegal at the time. And certainly not with Trini Lopez, who was too young at the time.)

Funnily enough, the Andrews Sisters had a big following in Germany, too, due to another great hit, '*Bei Mir Bist Du Schön*', which they said meant '*I Think You're Grand*' or '*Surrender at Once British Johnny*', depending on which country they were singing in at the time. The Andrews Sisters finished the war with another smash, '*Rum and Coca-Cola*', an infectious calypso song about G.I.s turning all the local girls into street walkers. *Hmm.* Whose side were you on, Andrews Sisters?

The Big Band Era: This *really* got out of hand as the bands got bigger and bigger. Benny Goodman and Tommy Dorsey tried to keep it under control, but by the time Glenn Miller arrived they had to wait for World War Two to begin to recruit enough men for the trombone sections alone.

The Big Bands were not only big but they were *long*. Once Gene Krupa played a drum solo on '*Sing, Sing, Sing*' that lasted for the entirety of 1943. Buddy Rich was the only man who could play faster than Krupa; they went through drumsticks so fast that Goodman had to hire a special lumberjack just to maintain the wood supply.

Some of the bandleaders, like Tommy Dorsey, had no personality whatsoever; but others, like Artie Shaw, were so full of personality they could barely conduct themselves in public, let alone the band. Artie usually had three nervous breakdowns before he had even begun *'Begin the Beguine'*.

Despite sterling work with *'Frenesi'* and the perhaps prophetically named *'Nightmare'*, Artie decided his work was not perfect enough and so, being a perfectionist, then quit the business to write books about his personal psychological discoveries. These sold surprisingly well, mainly because the people buying them thought they would find out how on earth Artie landed Lana Turner, but Shaw gave up writing to be moody full-time from 1954.

The Big Band Era had ended long before that, The Medium Band Era was a complete fizzer and soon the sanity of Small Combos returned (see below).

The Dave Brubeck Quartet: Now this was more like it. Just four chaps, all of whom played wonderfully well and no Troublesome Girl Singers who would inevitably leave to date Sinatra, or Troublesome Boy Singers, who would inevitably be beaten up by Sinatra for sounding a little *too* good. The Dave Brubeck Quartet played a new thing called 'Cool Jazz' that was mathematical yet spritely and every standard they touched now sounded exceptional.

Then, disaster struck with the incredible hit *'Take Five'*. The disaster was that this was the *sole* original that Dave Brubeck did not write himself, instead his alto-sax player Paul Desmond came up with it in about five minutes, which was also about how long it took for Desmond to earn a million bucks from the publishing royalties alone.

The Quartet's playing changed from Cool to Frosty, and by the time they recorded *Live at Carnegie Hall* the audience had to wear thermal long johns to make it through the performance without frostbite.

The Miles Davis Quintet: At least one player cooler than Dave Brubeck, they recorded the greatest jazz album of all time: *Kind of Blue*. The brilliant Bill Evans was the piano player! The genius John Coltrane was the sax player! And bloody Miles Davis was on trumpet! (Yes, this should have been clear from the name of the group, but Davis was a taciturn character, who often chose to spend entire albums and concerts simply glaring at the sound engineer and cleaning his spit valve.)

Miles realised that he could never top this album and spent the rest of his career being deliberately perverse and almost taunting his worshipping audience to leave (see *Dylan, Bob* for a more recent example of this behaviour). Still it was wonderful while it lasted and it lasts every time you pop on *Kind of Blue*, which we suggest every Senior does when they want to feel cool.

Wear a turtleneck and dark glasses and you will practically feel like you are in the band. Jazz cigarette highly recommended while listening, if you get my drift.

The Great American Songbook

This was not actually a single book by one person, despite what Irving Berlin thought. Many brilliant writers contributed to the *Great American Songbook*, which was lucky for Rod Stewart as he ran out of songs after '*Do Ya Think I'm Sexy?*' but made a motza rasping this stuff in the 21st century. The following are some great composers of said *Songbook* that all Seniors should know:

George and Ira Gershwin: But mainly George, really. Let's be honest, there were no lyrics in '*Rhapsody in Blue*' or '*An American in Paris*' and they were not missed. Although Gene Kelly was in *An American in Paris* and he did a charming rendition of '*I Got Rhythm*' with those French kids, so points for Ira there.

The tell was that George died in 1937 and Ira wrote sod all

for the next 50 years apart from the theme to *The Flintstones*. That is not quite true, but he did collect enormous royalties for doing nothing for half a century. Nice work if you can get it, as somebody wrote.

Cole Porter: Unlike every other songwriter he was born loaded and stayed that way. Was a member of the Whiffenpoofs at Yale and got rid of the Whiffen part as soon as he graduated. An extraordinarily talented man, Porter was brilliantly witty in his lyrics, effortlessly charming in his magical melodies and seemed to have every gift the Gods could bestow. Then a horse fell on him. He was riding the horse at the time, but, still, it was a surprise and led to over 47 operations on his legs, arms and torso, none of which were entirely successful.

Nevertheless, he managed to write *'Night and Day'*, *'You're the Top'*, *'Begin the Beguine'*, *'I've Got You Under My Skin'*, *'Anything Goes'* and about a hundred other standards. And yet *you* complain because your lower back hurts and don't feel quite up to raking the leaves today. Get a grip. Like the *beat beat beat* of the tom-tom, you shall finish the job before the evening shadows fall.

Oh, one other thing about Cole Porter – a lot of people thought he joined the French Foreign Legion, but he didn't. He did entertain a Legion of Foreign Frenchmen but that is not appropriate content for this book.

Rodgers and Hart: Rodgers wrote the music, Hart wrote the words and together they wrote some of the best stuff ever, including *'My Funny Valentine'* (not funny at all, really, but a very beautiful song), *'Bewitched, Bothered and Bewildered'*, *'My Heart Stood Still'*, *'Mountain Greenery'* and *'Have You Met Miss Jones?'*. You would think this would make any duo happy, but then Hart caught Rodgers mid-composition with Oscar Hammerstein and all hell broke loose.

Hart chased Rodgers all through Oklahoma and most of the South Pacific before giving up after hearing 'Some Enchanted Evening' and agreeing it was pretty damn good. Luckily for both, Hart died shortly thereafter (this was to be expected as Hart was always short, 5'1" actually, but he had hoped to die taller).

Irving Berlin: Wrote nearly everything. Seriously. 'Cheek to Cheek', 'Easter Parade', 'Putting on the Ritz', 'White Christmas', 'Anything You Can Do (I Can Do Better)', 'Change Partners', 'There's No Business Like Show Business', 'God Bless America', 'Blue Skies', 'A Pretty Girl Is Like a Melody' and that was just on a Tuesday.

Berlin was so prolific and so great that other composers seriously suspected he was employing anonymous songwriters to come up with his stuff. What made it even more infuriating is that Berlin *could not read or write music*! Irving could only play it on the piano and a musical Amanuensis would then *take it down* and *run it down* to Tin Pan Alley for the highest bidder. (The Alley was not literally made of Tin Pans, although it frequently sounded that way if Ethel Merman was demoing the songs.)

As well as being brilliant, Berlin was an immensely practical man. When his first wife died, did he blub? Yes he did, but he also immediately wrote the beautiful standard 'What'll I Do?' to commemorate her. Then, when he met his next wife, some months later, he wrote another beautiful standard, 'Always', to celebrate her. Unfortunately the second Mrs Berlin remained healthy for the next 50 years, or who knows how many more classics he might have written?

Berlin wrote the *defining* popular songs for both Easter and Christmas and he was Jewish! All Seniors must bow to Irving Berlin, he was a freakish talent, loving family man, incalculably wealthy and, most importantly, lived to the age of 101 and thus is a Senior Role Model.

CHAPTER 10

Senior Moments in Grandparenting

Senior Grandparenting: A Practical Guide

Becoming a Grandparent is both a delightful and horrifying experience for many Seniors. The horrifying part usually happens just after the pregnancy is announced, when a fellow grown up, usually one of your own smirking Adult Children, ruins the happy moment by referring to you as 'Grandma' or 'Grandpa' for the first time and you can literally feel the last illusions of your youth being stripped away in a second; a dreadful reverse-Dorian Gray moment that no Grandparent can avoid or forget.

This is the official moment when you stop being 'Late Middle-Aged' and now become a Senior. It is no good telling yourself that Mick Jagger is also a grandparent: Mick is currently seducing a Brazilian model in her late twenties in between gigs and groupies at Madison Square Garden; you are just old.

Yes, you were so used to be being a Mother or Father that now hearing the prefix 'Grand' can be a shock and initially annoying, much like a Paul Simon album released after *Graceland*. However, like Mr Simon's latter oeuvre, you will eventually get used to it and come to quite enjoy it. In any case, the delightful part is having a lovely New Baby to play with, one that will not grow up and blame all its personal failings on you unlike some ungrateful children we could name.

As every Senior knows, Grandparenting is a competitive sport. Your grandchild will usually have another rival set of grandparents, also anxious to spend time with the tiny tots while they are young and adorable in the key Pre-Stroppy-Teen years. The first battle to win is 'What Shall We Call Ourselves?'

For the love of God, jump in quickly and claim the premier titles 'Grandpa' and 'Grandma/Granny' quickly; a good tactic is to turn up at the hospital with those titles inscribed on a porcelain set of something Peter Rabbit as soon after the birth as possible. 'Nana' and 'Papa' are also acceptable. Try to dodge the following second-tier titles:

'Grampy': Sounds like one of the Seven Dwarves that didn't make the cut.

'Gammy' or 'Gam-Gam': First title sounds like one of your legs doesn't work; second like neither works.

'Maw-Maw' and 'Paw-Paw': Both sound like 1950's sex pest complaints. *'He maw-mawed me throughout the newsreel, officer. The paw-paw began during the second feature and entirely spoilt the opening of* "Genevieve".'

The above titles, although not optimal, all clearly acknowledge the fact that you *are* Grandparents and therefore Officially Senior. Some Seniors try to dodge this reality by using foreign grandparent titles. This is acceptable and charming if you are say, Danish or Hungarian, but if you are Anglo Boomers it is a transparent act of vanity and age-cowardice that is beneath you.

You are fooling nobody and your fellow Seniors pity you. We have no sympathy for Sneaky Seniors who hide behind the following ridiculous aliases:

'Nonna and Nonno': Spanish/Italian. Makes you sound like a novelty folk act from the early '60s who sang the original version of *'Those Were the Days'*. Either that or two of Geppetto's less successful wooden boy experiments. Patently ridiculous.

'Yiayia and Pappous': Greek and good luck getting away with it unless you look like Zorba. 'Couscous and Troy' would sound less silly.

'Avo and Vovo': Portuguese. Sounds like you are trying to sell biscuits door to door or eating Avocado in a boxy car from Sweden.

'Baba and Gigi': These are Ukrainian grandparent titles apparently. We have no idea which one is the male; both are extremely silly and together you will sound like a rather unsavoury sequel to a Leslie Caron movie.

Speaking of unsavoury, have you seen the original *Gigi* lately? It's a film about grooming a courtesan in her mid-teens which also features Maurice Chevalier at full leer singing *'Thank Heaven for Little Girls'* while ogling underage women walking near the Louvre. Arguably his most tasteless career move, including collaborating with the Nazis.

My Fair Lady is also a bit suss when you think about it. Henry Higgins would not fare well in the 'Me Too' era or any Human Resources department. Shoves marbles into an employee's throat, has her clothes burnt while she is forcibly bathed, even the 'romantic' ending has Higgins telling Eliza to fetch his slippers.

(What he intends to do with the slippers remains ambiguous but, still, a bit of an eyebrow raiser.)

Quite a lot of 'grooming' going on in beloved musicals actually: *Daddy Long Legs* the most obvious one, but even *An American in Paris* has its moments. (Both those films featured Leslie Caron, too, what was going on with her?) As for *Seven Brides for Seven Brothers*, it is a jolly film about mass kidnapping and enforced marriage which features an entire song enthusing about the Rape of the Sabine Women. Yes, the film had a brilliant barn-raising dance sequence and Howard Keel has a lovely singing voice, but we are more comfortable when he is singing about oh what a beautiful morning it is and the corn being as high as an elephant's eye, rather than harmonising about how women secretly want to be abducted at gunpoint.

Anyway, like many Seniors, we've strayed from the point, which is: cut these disguise names out. You are a *Grandma* or a *Grandpa*, calling yourself Gub-Gub and Ging Gang Gooley is not helping things. Accepting the title with grace is the best course for the Sensible Senior.

Becoming The Preferred Grandparents

Your children will tell you they treat both sets of Grandparents equally. This is a lie, and one Seniors recognise easily because it is the same sort of lie you told your children when you said, 'We don't have a favourite, we love you all equally.' The truth invariably is: mostly the oldest, sometimes the youngest, never the middles.

When it comes to becoming the Preferred Grandparents the trick is simple: behave like a zesty welfare officer and *remove the children from the premises.*

You get the grandchild all to yourself, nobody is there to see the sugar treats you feed them to ensure their love, and you give the Grateful New Parents a break and glimpse of sanity. Return the child three hours later when it has fallen asleep and you will be welcomed with garlands as though you have just retaken the Champs-Élysées.

Working in concert with Zoo, the Cinema, the Beach and TimeZone, you can become the Preferred Grandparents in no time. (Avoid the Bowling Alley: it looks like fun but they will inevitably drop the bowling ball on their foot or yours and there will be tears before bedtime.)

Amateur Grandparents will offer to 'lend a hand' and get drawn into the bedlam and seemingly Jackson Pollock-inspired hovel that is your once house-proud daughter-in-law's current hellish domain. Yes, yes, we know that you have sworn a blood oath to *Never Behave the Way That Your Mother-In-Law Behaved To You* but trust us, you will not be able to help yourself and will be making pointed remarks like, 'Goodness, is that the *same* peanut butter stain on your dress as yesterday or is it a fresh one?'

These remarks may be directed to either your daughter-in-law or your grandchild; the result will be the same, a blood-curdling glare followed by a few choice words and rather explicit if anatomically difficult directions you might care to follow.

Now this is not to say that you cannot have some Senior Fun while visiting your Adult Children and watching them deal with their own offspring. Every time a grandparent hears their child telling a grandchild *'Because I said so'* an Angel gets its wings.

As long as you keep a poker face that would impress Wild Bill Hickok you are free to enjoy the spectacle of reality hitting your children and their spouses smack in the face (often with a rewashable nappy that they insisted on purchasing because it was good for the environment. Not good for the immediate environment of the laundry room, which smells like poop, but again this is a fact you can observe, but not make observation *on*).

As a Silent Senior, you should not feel guilty at watching this delicious spectacle unfold (which is more than can be hoped of the nappy at this stage.) Why? Because you endured months of watching your children read books all entitled *How to Raise Your Children Properly (Which Is More Than Your Parents Did)* and *What To Expect That Your Stupid Parents Didn't* and all the other smug, passive-aggressive, Anti-Senior Parenting Bibles that are inhaled by the naive chumps that you brought up.

These tomes are all aggressively highlighted and helpfully verbally summarised for your retrospective benefit in a wistful 'Ah, what might have been' tone by the Expectant Couple. Oh, how differently *they* shall do things as they perfectly raise the world's first perfect infant since the baby Buddha. As Seniors know, there is nothing quite so irritating as being patronised by people whose bottoms you used to wipe. (No wonder the staff at Nursing Homes always look so cross.)

Remember to remain on your guard and stick to 'I don't remember' if they ask you any leading questions like: 'Did you make me use a dummy?' (*Make them!* They used to suck your thumb like a vampire after you dipped it into two fingers of Scotch and then they went out like a light. Tell no one.)

As Seniors will recall, back in our day there was only one book, written by Doctor Spock. God knows how he found the time, if memory serves Captain Kirk used to keep him pretty busy on the *Enterprise*, but it was pretty good stuff. Doctor Spock was anti-spanking, at least when it came to children, we think an exception might have been made for Lieutenant Uhura. Doctor Spock was also very big on 'reasoning' with children; although as previously mentioned the reason usually became '*Because I Said So*'.

Supplementary Senior Advice: Reading to Grandchildren

Be careful, many of the beloved books you kept from your own childhood are either staggeringly boring or staggeringly racist. Both in the case of *Biggles Massacres The Congo Just For Kicks*.

When it comes to race, *The Five Chinese Brothers* and *The Story About Ping* are both on the '*hmm…*' list and, charming as the Tiger Pancake ending is, *Little Black Sambo* is definitely out unless you want a quick visit from social services. As for Billy Bunter, apart from the fat shaming and binge eating, you will commit at least seven racial vilification offences by just reading out the names of his school chums at Greyfriars.

Enid Blyton wrote at least 700 books for children. They have done their best to give her a scrub for modern eyes, but if you retain any original editions you will be amazed at how many policemen were called Mr Gollywog. Oh, and if you want a real shock, try reading *The Story of Doctor Dolittle*, which literally features the idiot black Prince Bumpo having his face bleached white at his own request to be a proper person at last. Good luck paraphrasing your way out of that one.

When it comes to the boredom front, we will be impressed if you can struggle through even the first three chapters of *Blinky Bill* or *Seven Little Australians*. Even *Alice's Adventures in Wonderland* is bloody hard going; you need a good understanding of Whig politics of the 19th Century, a Fine Arts degree and a protractor to explain half the jokes and by then you will have given up and popped on the Disney Film Version.

Dr Seuss is almost always a safe pair of hands, but when you read *Green Eggs and Ham* you will want to strangle him, as it goes on forever with no mercy. You *could not, would not* cut this down? He *could not, would not* apparently and it will take you twenty minutes to plough through as Sam I Am makes it thoroughly clear that he does not like Green Eggs *and* Ham. (Spoiler Alert: he changes his mind at the end. Thanks for wasting our time, Seuss.)

CHAPTER 11

Senior Moments in Exercise

IN OUR YOUTH, THERE WAS NO SUCH THING AS 'EXERCISE'; EVEN Olympic Athletes were viewed with suspicion if they actually trained or tried hard, including during the race. (A bit of slow-motion running along the beach was allowed for the opening credits of stirring films, but not in real life.)

The closest thing to exercise that Seniors of the Past did was to 'Take their Constitutional', an august term for an extremely slow walk that usually passed by at least two open Pubs. Exercise, like Chapel, was a punishment one endured twice a week at school but it was given up with relief and relish upon maturity.

Apart from sport there simply was *no* exercise for adults. (Very occasionally a Medicine Ball was thrown at you, but this was before doctors had worked out medicine was best delivered in pill form.)

Sadly, in Modern Times, due to the relentless advice/bullying of our Friends, Spouses and Busybody Physicians, Seniors are often forced to endure some form of exercise. Please observe the following guidance and notes to avoid looking more ridiculous than necessary.

Jogging: This was known as *'cross country'* when we were at school and we hated it then, too. Now that most of the country has been sold off, only the cross bit remains and you can watch invariably furious young business people jogging through any major city at lunchtime. (*Where* do they shower? Why are they so cross? *Do* they shower? When do they have lunch if they spend their lunch hour jogging? Are they cross *because* they haven't had lunch? These are but five of the questions the Sensible Senior will ponder as they avoid emulating their example.)

Jogging is not recommended for the Senior, as it is particularly hard on the joints and the dignity. (Dencorub will help the former but do nothing for the latter.) If you must jog, do it at dawn or dusk; Seniors spotted jogging in daylight hours will inevitably be stopped by younger 'helpful' joggers who say *'Are you alright?'* or the even more infuriating *'Good for you!'*, departing with a thumbs up at speed as you are left to slow and steadily lose the race and the will to live.

Oh, and much the same way that Vegetarians never seem to mention that Hitler was a devout vegetarian for obvious reasons, Joggers are also very careful never to mention that the man who popularised jogging, Jim Fix, dropped dead while jogging. God rarely indulges in such obvious irony, so we should perhaps pay attention when he does. Feel free to bring up the fate of Jim Fix to any jogger, it will give them something to think about during their next lunchbreak to help them be furious.

Tai Chi: Increasingly popular with Seniors as it involves slow movement and a trip to the park, but you could be doing this without the Tai Chi bit and have more time to feed the ducks.

Everybody doing Tai Chi looks like they are auditioning to be bad Marcel Marceau impersonators. To be fair so did Marcel Marceau for the last 20 years of his endless career. How many retirement tours could one man have? (*Walking Against the Wind* was also accompanied by a fair amount of real wind during the Master's latter tours, which somewhat spoilt the atmosphere in more ways than one.)

Speed Walking: This used to only be performed as you stormed out of a dinner party during dessert after striking your Husband after he ogled the Hostess one too many times and said, 'My God, Stephanie, you're a *striking* woman!' Now you can see women doing it everywhere, their hands moving upwards at a rate many Go-Go Dancers would envy.

Speed Walking is a lot like Speed Dating, it becomes more depressing the more you do it and will probably end up with you alone in your apartment eating ice cream. Stick to Regular Walking, which can also be done in Regular Clothes; a great advantage as they are far more form flattering than the tight leotards sported by many optimistic but unwise Senior Exercisers.

Yoga: Formerly known as '*stretching*', then they added some sitar music from one of the George Harrison tracks that clogged up the later Beatles albums and it became a 45 minute class. Quite relaxing actually, but you will have to endure a lot of talk about 'Chakras' which are in permanent need of 'centreing' and 're-aligning' (presumably back to the 'centre').

The only Chakra that we knew was Chakra Kahn, who was never in need of centreing, she was bloody marvellous, made Shirley Bassey sound like she was whispering.

Zumba: One of Mowgli's advisers from *The Jungle Book*. Invented an expensive form of stationary dancing that counted as exercise in the 2000's. Fun, but one had to be careful of stance positioning or *Zumba* could accidentally become *Gropa* and you would be in a lawsuit in a *Moma*.

Aqua Aerobics: Supposedly this is Aerobics performed in the pool. These people are all kidding themselves. Aqua Tai Chi more like, except the soundtrack is *Hooked on Classics* blaring through the slightly wet boombox perched perilously close to the edge of the pool. If only you had an actual hook to hand you could drown that album in a second.

Spin Class: People have to be *taught* how to spin? You turn in a circle. Ridiculous. Take the advice of a well-known carpenter from Nazareth who advised his disciples to 'Consider the lilies, they toil not, neither do they spin'. (No, not Richard Carpenter, it was Jesus from Sunday School.) Funnily enough, a lot of Spin Class instructors are called Lily, one of those oddly self-fulfilling professions, like Butchers whose last name is Ham.

Pilates: Went to uni with Laertes and Hamlet. Also came up with this scam. Pilates is essentially Yoga without the new age music and they say 'Core' all the time instead of 'Chakra'. Not to be confused with Pontius Pilates, a far more painful form of exercise where you had to carry a wooden cross up a hill and then get nailed to it. (Not to be blasphemous, but we do note in most pictures the Lord does have fantastic abs and a waistline that even Mary Tyler Moore would envy.)

Bush Walking: A pleasant form of Senior Exercise, but, like getting a lift home with Teddy Kennedy, there is a high chance that the day may end with a Search Party being called. The Bush has the advantage of fresh air but the disadvantage of fresh snakes, most of whom look like sticks, including the *Brown Snake*, the *Stick Snake* and the *Did That Stick Just Move? Snake*.

The Jane Fonda Workout: Get married to either Roger Vadim or Ted Turner and you will lose weight too as you chase their various mistresses out of your house. Actually, she lost the most weight when she went on all those protest marches with Tom Hayden, who Seniors will remember was one of the *'Chicago 8'*. We preferred *Chicago Seven* (which from memory featured *'Does*

Anybody Really Know What Time It Is?' and *'Saturday in the Park'*) but they were both pretty good.

Senior Guide to the Gym

Like any Club that actively touts for business, Seniors should be wary of joining or even entering a Gym. The people at the front desk are always seductively fit and nice but when they say, 'You may stop your membership *at any time'* it does make you feel rather like 007 when the latest Arch Villain says, 'I assure you, Mr Bond, you are free to leave *at any time'*. Do *not* believe them.

Joining a Gym is like joining the Cosa Nostra or having a subscription to *Time Magazine*: there simply is no way out. (We are pretty sure Jim Fix is still a member of Fitness First and he jogged his last in 1984.) It is simply a question of careful wording: you *may* stop your gym membership, pigs *may* fly, your husband *may* fix the hoover without further prompting, etc.

Seniors are advised to be wary of the following Gym Activities:

Free Weights: A lie; they are not actually free, and you will be prosecuted if you succeed in getting them as far as your car.

The Rowing Machine: Slightly deceptive as the machine does nothing, you have to do the rowing bit.

The Dumbbell: Name applies equally to those who use it too frequently. Often people using Dumbbells stare at themselves in the mirror while doing so. Cats do this too (the mirror staring, not the Dumbbells. Outside of a *Looney Tunes* cartoon we have neither seen a feline make use of, or be struck by, a dumbbell, or an Anvil helpfully labelled '1000 TONS' come to think of it. Sylvester really was a particularly unlucky feline.)

When asked why they are staring at themselves, Dumbbell Users will reply that they are *'maintaining form'* not *'I am a shameless narcissist entranced by my hypnotic beauty'*, which they would if you jabbed them with Truth Serum.

Hot Yoga: It simply means the room temperature is high; no supermodels will be present.

The Treadmill: Exactly what it says, a metaphor made into the dullest form of exercise imaginable. The Treadmill is a wonderful machine for people who enjoy walking while staying in exactly the same place. It is the kind of exercise machine that Torquemada would have delighted in; after 15 minutes on it you will be prepared to renounce or denounce anything, starting with the bloody Treadmill.

To make things more exciting you can use a 'program' on the Treadmill that, wait for it, makes it *seem* like you are walking up a hill. (Or you could you just *leave the gym* and *walk up a hill*, for *free*.) We are surprised that Gyms do not offer similar grimly symbolic exercise devices; we are sure that a machine called 'The Grindstone' would be a very popular and painful nose exercise machine that would give much needed muscle tone to your sinuses.

The Kettlebell: Cruelly named because it gives you hope that someone is about to give you a nice cup of tea. They aren't. Instead, they will nicely invite you to put your back out by trying to lift this surprisingly heavy handbag-like torture device. Doesn't work as a bell, either, why did they call it that? We suppose 'Surprisingly Heavy Handbag-Like Torture Device' might have given the game away too soon.

When in the Gym, Seniors must be careful to observe Gym Etiquette. This is not like regular etiquette, such as always passing the Port to the left or standing when a lady joins the table; no, Gym Etiquette means 'wiping your sweat off a device after you use it'. This sounds obvious and disgusting but you would be amazed at the number of fights, accusations and duels at 50 paces Sweat Arguments take up at the Gym.

It wouldn't matter if King Solomon and Rumpole of the Bailey were watching who wipes off the Rowing Machine 24 hours a day, 23 of those hours would still be spent with people theatrically sighing and re-wiping off the seat whilst muttering dark oaths before they begin their precious turn.

As you know, Seniors are often correctly thought to have poor memories, so if, like us, you live in terror of Forgetting to Wipe, just make sure to carry a sopping-wet terry-towelling cloth clipped conspicuously to your waist at all times. People will be too revolted to even dare ask if you left the Elliptical in the manner in which you found it.

Oh, Seniors should be aware that when you are at the Gym you will often be asked by the staff *'Can you feel the burn?'* in a gleeful tone as though they are all enthusiastic pyromaniacs at a bonfire convention. What they mean is *'Are you in pain?'* Apparently, this means that the exercise is working. Again, it is very Torquemada, although at least when he burnt heretics he did not charge them a monthly membership fee.

CHAPTER 12

Senior Moments in Scandals

YES, WE KNOW THAT YOUNG PEOPLE THINK THEY LIVE IN AN exciting time for 'scandals' – the world is full of deliberately leaked Celebrity Sex Tapes, 'stolen' nude photos of aspiring Famous Actresses (meant only for the eyes of their partner and publicist) and hastily deleted 'controversial' Tweets – but the young have no idea what *real* scandal is. Take a juicy walk down Filthy Memory Lane as we examine the *best* Senior Scandals.

The Profumo Affair: This one had everything – Russian spies, sexy call girls, nude sexy Cabinet Ministers (yes, they did exist back then), Dentists drugging everyone (to be fair, this happened every time you had a tooth pulled in the Sixties, although Mandy Rice-Davies was seldom there dressed as a nurse and more is the pity), whips, chains, Douglas Fairbanks Jnr. (allegedly) and (allegedly) half of the extended Royal Family including most of the Corgis. It was hot stuff. Even the names were hot. 'Christine Keeler' still sounds like a Kama Sutra position for the exceptionally limber, which turned out to be not that far from the truth.

It was tremendous fun and led to several resignations, many highly profitable assignations for Ms Keeler and some very snippy breakfast interrogations for the Duke of Edinburgh. Every morning one would read a new delicately worded article in the paper describing how British High Society was essentially Sodom and Gomorrah with more brylcreem.

The Profumo Affair led to a) the fall of the Macmillan Government and b) record sales for that sexy chair that Christine Keeler sat backwards on. Not very good ergonomically, but the curves made it worthwhile.

In Like Flynn: Errol Flynn, who had never exactly seemed to be a pipe and slippers family man, confirmed his Playboy image in spectacular fashion with a statutory rape case that knocked even the Führer off the front pages during the war. In 1942, when Errol had wisely decided to spend WW2 fighting the Nazis onscreen in L.A., two 17-year-old girls somehow managed to slip aboard Errol's famous sailing vessel *The Jolly Roger*. We tease, his yacht was actually called *Sirocco*, but rogering of a very consensual but also jolly statutory nature certainly took place with these seductive stowaways.

Errol claimed that firstly, he was unaware of the girls' actual ages (*semi-believable*); secondly, he was rolling drunk (*completely believable*); thirdly, he was Errol Bloody Flynn (*true*) and fourthly, that the girls were hookers and he was being set up for blackmail. The jury agreed with the third and fourth bits.

Errol was acquitted and luckily the court case did not affect his reputation as he had successfully spent the entire 1930's in Hollywood ensuring that he did not have one. In a strange coda, many years later it was claimed that Errol Flynn was a Nazi Spy. We have no wish to be unkind to a fellow Australian's acting skills, but Errol could barely pull off playing a Travel Agent on film, let alone a Double Agent in real life.

Good-looking fellow, though. Got expelled from Shore for fooling around with the safely overage school Matron. Both scandals involved the Poop Deck but this is *not* that sort of book and, unlike Errol, we don't want to go into it.

Ingrid Bergman Getting Pregnant: While she wasn't married! All right, times are different now but it *was* a big scandal back then, especially as she had just played a nun in *The Bells of St. Mary's* with Bing Crosby. Bing was not the father, he was far too busy thrashing his children and usually left such activities to Bob Hope; in this case, however, the seductive cad in question was Italian Film Director Roberto Rossellini. To make matters worse, Rossellini was married, something that Ingrid was not aware of, having neglected to read the subtitles.

Anyway, their daughter grew up to be Isabella Rossellini. (Well, she was always Isabella Rossellini, even when she was small, but she wasn't in *Blue Velvet* then so you didn't care, did you?) Once grown up, Isabella Rossellini also dated a director, Martin Scorsese, who dated Liza Minnelli who dated and married anybody, including Peter Allen. You would think being the daughter of Judy Garland would have blessed you with a pretty good Gaydar but apparently not.

Would this tangled web have all been avoided if Ingrid Bergman had just married Rick instead of getting on the plane with Paul Henreid? Probably not, but we and Humphrey Bogart often wished she did.

Superman Kills Himself: No, this is not the new edgy plot of the increasingly miserable DC film universe, this *actually happened.* George Reeves, who played the Man of Steel on TV in the 1950's with the aid of chest foam to help with the suit and the aid of gin to get through the dialogue, astonished the world by apparently taking his own life with the aid of a speeding bullet to the head. But was it suicide or *murder?* The fact that the L.A. Police did not even bother to question Lex Luthor made many of us suspicious.

Other people began to wonder when it was revealed that George Reeves was a bit of a Superman in the sack with the wives of various Mafiosi and MGM executives (it was often difficult to tell them apart, which led to a hit being ordered on Shirley Temple. Fortunately the order was misunderstood and the hit turned out to be *The Littlest Colonel* with Bill 'Bojangles' Robinson doing that lovely staircase dance with her).

Oddly enough, the other handsome chap who played a nice Superman was Christopher Reeve, who suffered his own tragedy when he was cast in *Switching Channels* with Burt Reynolds and Kathleen Turner.

The singer Jim Reeves was also offered the part of Superman and, although he wisely turned it down, he died in a plane crash anyway, which was ironic as his biggest hit was the prophetic *'He'll Have to Go'*. Look, if your last name is Reeve or Reeves, just change it, okay? (Oh my God, I've just realised! *Keanu!* Someone check on that boy, I want to see *John Wick 4*.)

The Entire Kennedy Family: Non-stop scandal machine that briefly paused in between affairs and drownings to be re-elected. God knows how those boys found time for any work let alone paying attention during the Cuban Missile Crisis.

At one stage, things got so complicated even Jack and Bobby couldn't remember who was supposed to be having an affair with Marilyn Monroe and ended up using a round robin system devised by Teddy until Ms Monroe's unfortunate 'accidental' overdose. (The number of accidents that surround the Kennedy family, intentional or otherwise, are only rivalled by Mr Magoo.)

President Kennedy has been especially criticised for having the poor judgement to 'date' Judith Exner, the mistress of mobster Sam Giancana, but to be fair to JFK he was having affairs with half of the women in America at the time and the FBI simply could not read their resumes fast enough. Plus, the President was on so many pills he made Elvis look like a Christian Scientist.

The Kennedy Boys were so close they covered for each other even after they were dead. If you ever see *The New York Times* front page for the Moon Landing you will see a very small story in the bottom right corner with the miniature headline 'Senator Edward Kennedy Has Accident in Chappaquiddick'. Now *that* is timing.

Lana Turner's Daughter Stabs Johnny Stompanato: The scandal was terrific but got extra points for the last name 'Stompanato'. Johnny Stompanato (his *real name*! God, Billy Wilder would have *killed* to think of that name!) was a gangster who had been fortunate enough to date the lovely Lana Turner in 1958. One dark and stormy night Johnny also got a bit dark and stormy at Lana's Hollywood Hills mansion and ended up dead on the upstairs landing with a large carving knife in his stomach. Not since Artie Shaw had Lana Turner ended a relationship so decisively.

Many believed that Lana herself had done the deed, but like many thoughtful Hollywood mothers she let her 15-year-old daughter have a crack at acting, in this case on the witness stand, and the teenager was acquitted for committing justifiable homicide.

Did Lana do it? Who knows, but you can bet all her future boyfriends *never* stomped, were always on *best behaviour* around both the Turner girls, and that nothing sharper than a butter knife was ever let into the kitchen again.

Fatty Arbuckle: This scandal is too filthy and shocking to even begin to describe, we doubt you are even allowed to legally Google it. Let's just say Fatty took the 'Coke Is It!' slogan to realms undreamt of and at least one actress ended up dead. He was a bigger star than Charlie Chaplin and now you've never heard of him. (Of course you didn't really hear Chaplin either, he was a silent movie star, but you get the point.)

Believe it or not, but John Lennon's best friend from childhood, a fellow named Pete Shotton, started up a successful fast food burger chain restaurant in the UK in the 1980's named Fatty Arbuckles. We can only hope that they served Pepsi, for safety and hygiene reasons.

Lord Lucan: On 7 November 1974, the dashing and handsome 40-year-old John Bingham, the 7th Earl of Lucan, a professional gambler, bludgeoned his children's nanny to death in the basement of his Belgravia mansion and then vanished, supposedly with a briefcase of cash and diamonds, never to be seen again. Every three months he would be spotted in Bali, or acting as a Sherpa in the Himalayas, or in immaculate formal wear at a cocktail party in Kenya.

Lord Lucan became a far more exciting 'Where's Waldo?' for the entire world. It made every holiday a thrill; each vaguely tall beach bum would be given a careful once over as you walked by, followed by a barely *sotto voce* 'I think it's him' to check if it was Lord Lucan and whether he would make another run for it.

The mystery endures; he would be in his mid-80's by now, but if by any chance his Lordship is reading this work, do drop us a line and let us know where you are. Discretion assured, we are just curious.

The Elizabeth Taylor Scandals: Okay, this might take some time, and we are only going to give you the short versions. America's Sexpot Liz was married (frequently obviously) but in 1958 to the world's biggest movie producer, Mike Todd. (To be clear, the movies were big; Mike ran about 5'10"). Mike died in a plane crash whereupon Liz was comforted by Mike's best pal, the singing sensation Eddie Fisher, who was married to America's sweetheart, *Singing in the Rain* star Debbie Reynolds, and was also the father of Princess Leia, who, spoiler alert, married Han Solo.

Anyway, to the very, very recently widowed Mrs Todd, Mr Fisher was a *big* comfort, so big in fact that Liz decided to marry him next, which was unpleasant news for Debbie who had two under two at the time. Then, Liz and Eddie went to Rome where Liz was going to make the world's most expensive movie, *Cleopatra*, where she met the also-married-at-the-time Richard Burton. They then decided to marry each other, often on camera, which was fun at first but eventually even the cameraman ran out of patience and angles and the trailer alone was so over budget it bankrupted 20th Century Fox well into the 21st century.

Then Liz and Richard got divorced, then married again after she got the World's Biggest Diamond as her latest engagement ring, then she got divorced again (kept the ring, smart girl) then she went out with a guy called Bungalow Bill (not kidding) and then ended up marrying a construction worker she had met in rehab called Larry Fortensky.

Apart from that, she dated Ringo Starr, rode National Velvet to victory (this *may* have just been in a movie, but she totally sold it and she was 12!) and divorced Conrad Hilton Jnr. at the age of 21 for 'non-performance', shall we say. (If you could not perform with a 21-year-old Liz Taylor you were not only divorced you were declared legally dead. Even Liberace would have managed it, and we're pretty sure Rock Hudson and James Dean both did in between takes for *Giant*.)

To cap things off, when 9/11 happened, and this is 100% true, Liz was in New York, freaked out and hired a limo, which she drove all the way to Ohio with… Marlon Brando and Michael Jackson. Bloody Hell! We, and the tabloids of the world, miss Miss Liz, who was a great actress, a great beauty, a great sport and last of the true 'dames' and we salute her as the all-time champion of Senior Scandals.

CHAPTER 13

Senior Moments at Weddings

BACK IN THE DAY, WEDDINGS WERE PRETTY MUCH BY THE BOOK: a slightly hungover groom, rented morning suits, the bride wore white (and often deserved to) and it was held in a Church. My God, how things have changed, including God who barely gets a look-in at most ceremonies. Please observe this Senior Guide to Weddings to get through the day/evening/sunset commitment ceremony with a straight face and a bit of grace.

There may be many reasons for a Senior to attend a Wedding: apart from the free cake and booze, you are usually peripherally related to the Bride or Groom (or Brides or Grooms, as we say, things have changed), or you may have saved the Father of the Bride's life back in 'Nam (you would be surprised how often this explanation works on a slightly tipsy bridesmaid).

The first piece of bewilderment at a Modern Wedding for the Senior starts before it even begins with a 'Save the Date' card. This used to be called a 'Wedding Invitation'. Why don't you 'Save Some Time' and 'Save Some Paper' and just ask us?

Wedding Gifts: Like Meghan Markle, these things have now gotten completely out of hand. In the old days, the Happy Couple used to become ecstatic if you went to the trouble of getting them a double-sized toaster; now the 'Bridal Registry' reads like some jaded 19th century Rajah's birthday wish list.

Marble 'Island' Benchtops? Truffle Making Lessons? Kayaking 'Adventures'? We are surprised they left Fabergé eggs off the list. The Bride should be registered in a sanitarium if she thinks Seniors will fork out so she can assemble some eccentric Aladdin's Cave just for getting hitched.

The Senior Solution to such needless extravagance is simple: buy the cheapest thing on the registry, wrap carefully, but make sure *no card is included or attached*. Then when you get to the wedding, place your cheapo gift in the giant jumble of swag and rip the cards off five of the more expensive-looking presents (elaborate ribbons are the giveaway). Bin the cards and you have now, sadly, been 'lost in the shuffle'. You can experience smug Senior Satisfaction when you receive a suitably ambiguous thank you card from the Bride months later as she recovers from a bruised fibula that happened mid-Kayak.

Children at Weddings: Do not assume they are a forgotten nephew or some half-pint half-cousin, most of the time they belong to the couple who are about to be wed. Schoolground chants are not always 100% accurate but up until about 1978 *'First comes love, then comes marriage, then comes baby in a baby carriage'* held true. Now it's more like *'First comes sex, then came baby, waited four years to marry because they're lazy'*.

The clue to the fact that the children in question will soon be legally related to the Bride or Groom are a) they will wear white and b) their Non-Haircuts. For some reason, the unwed prefer to have their children's hair not be cut, instead it is lazily draped around their entire head like some sort of Minor Romantic Poet on a windy day, invariably covering at least two thirds of their face. It is usually impossible to guess whether they are a boy or a girl, if binary gender is still your bag.

On no account refer to the children as '*bastards*', however much their behaviour may justify the label. The descriptor '*remarkable*' will be suitably ambiguous if anyone asks for your opinion on the tots as they run down the aisle shrieking and deliberately throwing rose petals at the congregants' faces.

'Adorable, aren't they?'

'*They are remarkable.*'

Kilts: No, we don't know what happened, either, but now every second set of groomsmen dress as though they are about to launch into a spirited rendition of '*Mull of Kintyre*'. Apart from Sir Sean Connery, almost nobody has the knees to pull off wearing a kilt, and their kilts should be pulled off at the first opportunity.

I don't care if your name is Angus McTavish-Hootsmon, you are still not Scottish enough to justify wearing that outfit more than 50 miles from Loch Lomond. Wear a tuxedo for God's sake; it's your wedding day, not a *Braveheart*-themed fancy dress party.

(Some Seniors have theorised that there is some subconscious sabotage going on here: every Bachelor Boy gets cold feet, perhaps they think if the Bride has to look at their cold hairy knees as they walk down the aisle they might call it off. We would not blame these girls, you look ridiculous and your Sporran is facing the wrong way.)

The Venue: As we have said above, the venue used to be The Local Church. You know, the one you actually went to? Nowadays it can be anywhere from a beach, a winery, a golf course, or any other place where the photos look nice but where nobody can hear anything during the ceremony. This is especially true at beach weddings where the words '*What was that?*' are yelled far more often than '*I do*'.

Golf courses should also be re-thought as wedding venues, as many Grooms will find their eyes irresistibly drawn to the first tee instead of their Bride. (We know an empty golf course is the definition of male temptation, but even if you are the Third Groomsman, on no account ask the Bride *'Could I possibly get away with three holes before the reception?'*, or you may find yourself in one of the more spectacular sexual misunderstandings of your lifetime.)

Destination Weddings: Avoid, as the destination will invariably be the mystical tropical island of Near Bankruptcy. Young Couples, if you want to go to Waikiki or the Maldives for your honeymoon that is your affair (although you should not be having an affair on your honeymoon, give it a year at least). Do not expect Seniors to subsidise you by attending a ceremony so you can wangle some discount group rate on the quiet, we are *on to you*.

The Celebrant: Oh dear. In the beloved past that all Seniors wish still existed, usually one just had to watch a slightly bored Vicar, who had done a hundred of these ceremonies, and was anxious to get through the thing quickly because they were behind on this week's sermon *'Shall the Seed Fall on Stony Ground?'* It took five minutes tops, a quick reading of *'But if I have not love, I am become sounding brass'* etc. and we were already at the 'sign here' bit.

Now we have the 'Celebrant', which is not a cause for celebration. Regardless of age they are invariably New Age and would like to start off with several pieces of their favourite poetry, one of which is invariably from *The Prophet* by Kahlil Gibran. One of the good things about a Bible reading is that you get a warning as to how long this whole caper is going to go on for right up front, i.e. *'John, Chapter 2, verses 1–11'*. You would have to be a Prophet to guess correctly how much Kahlil Gibran you are going to have to swallow, especially as he never completes a sentence, let alone a thought, i.e.:

'Let there be togetherness in your spaces, and spaces in your togetherness, when love beckons, then follow love, though love's beckoning be full of spaces and your ending be but your beginning, and your beginning be but the ending of another beginning where love beckons etc. etc. ad infinitum.'

It's like Rod McKuen without the music or the endings. (If you ever wonder who exactly Kahlil Gibran was, he was a very clever chancer who wrote, *not* in the mystic east, but in Manhattan in the 1920's under the patronage of his secret mistress, a headmistress named Mary Haskell. Gibran died of cirrhosis of the liver, brought on by his alcoholism, brought on presumably by having to try to understand what on earth *The Prophet* was about.)

After Poetry Corner, the Celebrant will give you some of their general musings about marriage (the bride may have thought that this is her 'special day' but every day is a special day for a Celebrant) along with a few tips on 'keeping the flame of love *ever burning*' etc. (At this point you can literally hear all the already married couples' eyes *ever rolling*.)

After the Celebrant is done (for now) we come to the really hard part:

People Write Their Own Vows: When Seniors got married, the vows were the nice and simple – *Do you take him? Yep. Do you take her? Yep.* And we were done. These vows worked for two millennia. Now we all have to watch the Bride and Groom have an emotional breakdown in public, as they struggle through long, long pre-written spontaneous thoughts about how they met, their *'journey'* together (*read: multiple break-ups before settling*), and of course the compulsory ending about how they 'complete each other'. (If *they* complete each other, what are *we* doing here?)

Movie-going Seniors will recall that this 'completing each other' thing started in the entertaining Tom Cruise vehicle *Jerry Maguire* where an emotional Tom told Renée Zellweger at the climax of the film, '*You complete me*'. This was understandable as Renée Zellweger still looked like Renée Zellweger at that point and would have completed us too if we could get anywhere near her.

If we are really going to use Tom Cruise movie quotes to replace traditional vows, why not go with *A Few Good Men*? Doing the '*You want the truth? You can't handle the truth!*' speech after being asked 'Do you take this woman?' would make for a far more exciting wedding, although perhaps not for a lengthy marriage.

The Reception: As a Senior you will often find yourself the odd one out at a table of younger attendees. Do not let this intimidate you from making and dominating the conversation. As a Senior, you have now passed safely into your Anecdotage: the golden time when you can make up almost any story about the distant past and be believed. You will be *fascinating*.

Make a start by telling them about the time you saw The Beatles play in Hamburg. 'Back then, Paul played the piano, not the bass. My one regret is not taking up John's invitation to sit in on drums.' Then you can move to your peripheral involvement in the Moon Landing – 'Somebody had to hold those power cords together with their bare hands or Mission Control would just become static. I realised, at that exact moment, *that person was me*.'

And perhaps close with the time Steve McQueen fender bendered your MG while you were street racing for kicks in 'Cisco in the mid-'70s. Remember to observe the Senior Rule of Three; you can get away with three good fake anecdotes before anyone gets suspicious and starts to question you specifically about dates while using Google.

The Speeches: These at least have remained the same – semi-bawdy from the Best Man, sentimental and bit teary from the Maid of Honour. (Weddings are always pure hell for the Maid of Honour: their best friend is getting married first and therefore has 'won'; plus the Bride, subconsciously or otherwise, can never resist choosing dreadful dresses for her sad-sack retinue. We have seen some poor girls wearing 'outfits' so unflattering that they would make the young Renée Zellweger look like the current Renée Zellweger.)

The one person who really has to watch out here is the probable Senior: the Father of the Bride. Keep it short and sweet, you have not lost a daughter you have gained a son, etc. and do not throw in a 'fun': *'Free at Last! Free at Last! Thank God Almighty we are Free at Last!'*

Wedding Dancing: All Seniors should dance at a wedding just to show off that they actually can. Only about 20% of Millennials would be able to even recognise a Waltz, let alone do it. After the Bride and Groom 'dance', have a quick word to the Wedding Band and put them and the other juniors to shame with a quick Foxtrot, a Tango (if your back is still up to it), and then finish off with a medley of The Hully Gully, The Watusi and, as a concession to those under 50, The Twist, which along with The Hokey Pokey and The Macarena, remain the only dances that Non-Seniors are remotely capable of. Grab some cake, kiss the Bride and you are home free. (We advise two doses of Epsom Salts in the bath tonight, The Hully Gully had a few more gullies than you remembered.)

CHAPTER 14

Senior Conversation Starters: New Complaints

As a Senior you already have many things to complain about, starting with old favourites like your daughter-in-law, medications that don't work and how Test Cricket is being ruined. But why not try some new things and meet Similarly Annoyed Seniors in the process? Please try to engage the nearest Senior in conversation using one of the following complaints as an 'ice breaker'.

Department Store Clerks Who Refuse to Make Eye-Contact

They have now replaced waiters as masters of the art of ignoring their customers. You could set yourself on fire whilst singing the *'Anvil Chorus'* at David Jones and still not get that man at the sock counter to look up or, God forbid, actually help you. And that's another thing: *is it the sock counter?* The sections used to be clear in the old days, now it looks as though some half-soused interior design team with a lazy eye has just thrown things about randomly and then left, apparently taking the cash registers with them.

Loyalty Cards for Supermarkets

Honestly, you used to swear loyalty to your country and possibly your regiment and now you have to declare fealty to Woollies? No thank you. Feels like you are in the middle of the McCarthy Hearings when you are just trying to buy a tin of peaches.

Home Schooling

What on earth is going on? Back in the day only that poor boy in *The Secret Garden* and possibly a couple of the Mitford Sisters had lessons at home. Now every third urchin is at it. All those home-schooled children will never experience one of the great pleasures of adulthood: the thought that however bad your day is, at least you are not back at school.

Bank Tellers Who Call You By Your First Name

Cut it out. Just because you can see my bank balance, that is no reason to get chummy, you are not going to get any. 'Sir' or 'Madam' will suffice.

Men Wearing Sandshoes

The clue is in the name. Sandshoes are to be worn at the beach, not in a shopping centre, a restaurant or church. Women wear heels for goodness sake, the least any male over the age of 11 can do is wear grown-up shoes when they are out. Do you think Cary Grant would have ever been caught dead in a pair of sandshoes? Well, perhaps in *To Catch a Thief* but he was a cat burglar so he had an excuse.

The Post Office

My God, where to start? First, you have to beat your way through the White Elephant Stall that is nine-tenths of the place. Then you get the thrill of standing in a non-moving line listening to people loudly conduct various mundane financial transactions and paying utility bills at a length and boredom level that would defy even a Russian novelist.

If you retain the will to live and reach the front of the queue, the staff seem genuinely surprised if you want to buy some stamps and positively startled if you want to mail something. Bring back red pillar boxes, fire everybody and begin again please.

Shop Assistants Who Tell You the Price is 'Just'

'It's just $64.99.' Oh, is it just? In my day three pounds eight shillings was considered quite a lot, and you'd think twice before handing a tenner over to anyone if you weren't buying a car, and now 65 smackers is 'just', apparently. If you could *just* tell me the price and *just* stop adding your scripted opinion on how cheap that is, that would be *just* wonderful.

Workers at Grog Shops Who Tell You to 'Have a Good One'

I don't wish to have a 'good one', I will be having a *quiet* one at home watching *Brief Encounter*, actually, not that it's any of your business.

Bank Emergency Lines with Operators Who Ask 'Can You Remember Your Password?'

If I could remember my password I wouldn't have called and gradually progressed in your infernal queue for 26 minutes. Idiot.

And I don't care what the 'Memory Prompt' on your screen says, the name of my first pet was 'Mr Jingles'. Got run over by the milk truck, thanks for bringing that memory up.

Hard Glasses Cases

Why on earth do they make all hard cases for glasses snap shut so fast you almost lose a finger every time? And then you need the forearm strength of Arnold Schwarzenegger to prise the damn things open again. All that's in there is a pair of spare glasses, not the contents of Fort Knox. Get a grip, glasses case manufacturers, or rather, don't get a grip.

'Invisible' Hearing Aids

Not actually invisible, just invisible enough so that if you take one out for four seconds and put it down you'll never find it again. Yes, people can't instantly see that you are deaf but I'm pretty sure they'll figure it out when you yell in the restaurant "Can anyone see my bloody hearing aid?"

Expiry Dates on Hot English Mustard

Really? I have a bottle bought during the height of the Raj that is still going strong.

Michael Bublé

Yes, his Christmas Album is very nice, but as for the rest of his stuff, people are aware that you can still buy Frank Sinatra CDs, aren't they? So what are we doing?

CHAPTER 15

Senior Moments in Home Improvement

A Don't-Do-It-Yourself Guide for Seniors

In times of yore, Seniors would do practically nothing around the house. If household repair or maintenance were needed, 'a little man' would be called. (Most often they were not little, they were large, drank surprising amounts of tea, never stopped talking, and had a moody looking younger assistant who, for some unspecified reason, would *not be allowed inside the house*.)

As time went on, the 'little man' evolved into the slightly more dignified sounding 'Handyman'. (Ironically, they were not handy, they were permanently absent, always *just finishing off another job*, which meant that your job wouldn't even get a look-in for at least a fortnight.)

Oddly enough, the 'little man' has made a comeback: he now only exists to 'fix' Computers for Seniors and teach them how to turn on their Televisions, tasks that are either beneath the Handyman or too complicated for them, we are not entirely sure which. And it is Television, or rather specifically the Home/Lifestyle/Renovation shows that plague it, that have led to a grave danger for Aspirational Seniors: the curse of Home Improvement.

Much like the Seniors that now live in them, Homes used to be settled and done with change by the time they were 35.

Occasionally there was loose talk of a 'Sunroom' being created, but this usually just meant that you couldn't afford to buy proper curtains yet for the hallway.

Now every room, from the kitchen to the bedroom, is in constant danger of 'improvement', with a squadron of Architects, Builders, Designers, Building Designers, Renovators and Inspectors who will appear in your home and refuse to leave until you don't recognise it. To survive, pay attention to the following:

Architects and Builders: The Hatfields and the McCoys of Home Improvement, each primarily exists to antagonise and defy the other.

The Architect is happiest when divorced entirely from the constraints of reality, explicit instructions and your budget, writing in white on blue pieces of cardboard. The Builder, in turn, is required by law to shake his head sadly and sigh as he holds up and examines each of the Architect's proposals, as though readying and steadying himself to give you some particularly grim news about a cloudy area on an X-Ray.

Do not worry: this is an ancient tradition and they will soon enough come to an accommodation, which is to do what they like to *your* accommodation because you have already given up and decided to '*leave it to the professionals*'. This is an excellent policy when it comes to hiring hitmen to eliminate your rivals, but not when it comes to getting the guest bedroom just as you would like it.

'Improvements' to Look Out For: Senior Tips to Preserve Your Home, Budget and Sanity

1. Building a Swimming Pool: First, and we can't emphasise this enough, do *not* build a swimming pool. You may as well buy a yacht. It will be slightly more expensive but at least you will see water within a year. However, all Seniors know that a pool is a guaranteed Grandchild Magnet, and as such is a valuable and irresistible weapon in the quest to become Preferred Grandparents.

If you do start building a Pool, you will notice as soon as the contract is signed that your pool building 'crew' vanishes like Houdini at the first threat of a) Rain or b) Sun (or 'Pre-Rain' as it is known in the building profession). The Builder himself will suddenly turn into an enigmatic sage who would rival Confucius. The following is a typical exchange:

You: When will the Pool be finished?
Builder: *It will be finished when it is finished.*
You: Right. Well, when will the concreting be done?
Builder: *It will be done when it is done.*
You: What is the sound of one hand clapping?
Builder: *I have no idea. You have been pre-billed per our instalment agreement for this meeting.*

Building a Pool is an exciting and endless process consisting of the following steps, which you can understand using our Senior Translator:

Excavation = Digging a big hole in your backyard and leaving it there (the dog used to do this for free *and* with some sense of purpose).

Steel Fixing = The crew is still fixing the excavation, Builder on vacation.

Concreting = You dream constantly of burying the Builder in some wet concrete if and when he ever returns.

External Plumbing = You get the first bill while standing outside and wet yourself while standing next to the big hole still in your backyard.

Fence Inspection = Using a third party to pay off the council inspector.

Pebble Interior = Fred Flintstone's daughter is inside.

All of these steps are expensive, but the Savvy Senior will be able to save money upon completion by filling the Pool with their own tears. Pools provide a lifetime of pleasure, for Pool Construction Companies.

You, on the other hand, will spend the remainder of your days leaf-scooping and discussing pH levels more than the average bio-chemist as your wife glazes over, unlike the Pebble Interior, which still leaks.

2. Bathrooms: Most bathroom renovations are bog standard, but there is one renovation that Seniors should be particularly wary of: the Art Deco Bathroom.

Architects for some reason are obsessed with restoring, transplanting and, we think if given the chance, marrying Art Deco bathrooms. Like you, when we think of Art Deco we think about Fred and Ginger doing '*The Continental*' on an improbably big nightclub dancefloor. We gave no thought to where Fred or Ginger used to go to relieve themselves between takes.

The hallmark of the Art Deco bathroom is '*original pink hexagon tiling*'. It remains very original in the sense that all subsequent designers abandoned it on the grounds of taste and the fact every time you sit on the loo it looks like you are stranded in an ocean of calamine lotion.

Leave Art Deco where it belongs, in the 1930's and in lovely old cinemas, and hire Bert Deco instead; he will build you a 21st century bathroom that actually works.

3. Kitchens: Sooner or later, one day the Senior Wife will remark that the Kitchen has become 'rundown and tatty'. Resist the temptation to say 'Just like its owners' or you'll find the back of your head meeting the Frying Pan at a remarkable velocity. Once Senior Ladies get it in their head to renovate the kitchen, just get out of their way. They have put up with a lot in their time, including you, so zip it.

The wise Senior Husband will use the Kitchen Reno as a 'Den Pro Quo', which is the only way you have a hope in hell of getting your ridiculous Man Cave spouse-approved. Both Seniors are advised to go along with this thing carefully, like it's a prisoner exchange at Checkpoint Charlie. If you both keep your nerve, don't scream, and resist the urge to say *'Really?'* at any point, then both parties can return to their respective territories alive and still married.

4. The Guest Bedroom: If you are a Senior Male, be very wary if your spouse suddenly becomes interested in creating a 'Guest Bedroom'. Due to the long established fact that you snore (*yes you do, of course you don't think you do, you can't hear it, etc.*), this so-called Guest Bedroom will soon turn into Your Bedroom. Think about it, how often do you have guests that you want to sleep over? Yes, perhaps back in the Seventies but times and the strength of STDs have changed since that simpler and more swinging time.

The Guest Bedroom is the Reverse Trojan Horse of Senior Marriage. Once inside the premises its true purpose will be unleashed and you will be ordered to totter groggily out of your Own Bedroom and into the 'Guest Bedroom' at 2 am every night because you snore (*yes you do, of course you don't think you do, you can't hear it, etc.*).

5. The Verandah or Deck: The difference between a verandah and a deck is simple, it's about $50,000. We're joking, it's much more than that. A deck is less expensive than a verandah as it requires no roof, but it more than makes up for that with its constant need for oiling, sanding, coating, coaxing, sweeping, painting, scrubbing, stripping and re-nailing. The late Joan Crawford was the only creature who required more yearly maintenance than a deck, and your deck has no juicy stories about Bette Davis that make it worth the trouble.

Home and Garden is quite enough, there is no need for the Senior to add a wooden wraparound. You are living in suburbia not on the *Ponderosa*, stop being so hearty and enjoy yourself.

6. Ladders: On no account, during any Home Improvement, Maintenance or even Gardening, should any Senior ever be up on a ladder. 'He was up on a ladder' is the sentence most frequently heard by the Admitting Registrar in any Emergency Room and also the explanation most often given to curious Undertakers.

Every Senior is initially cautious when they gingerly and carefully climb a ladder to start a task, but within minutes you start feeling strangely at ease, *leaning* soon leads to *holding on with just one hand* and shortly you'll be behaving as though you are one of the Flying Wallendas, before taking a short flight groundwards and landing on *your* wallenda at best.

We have always thought that there is something sinister and malevolent about ladders in general, particularly old ones, probably all those black cats that walked under them had some effect that science cannot yet understand. Lure the 'little man' away from rebooting your modem and get *him* to go up the ladder instead.

It is not a coincidence that Ladders are also inexorably linked to the most common and disastrous form of Senior Home Improvement...

7. Painting: It seems such a simple thing to just 'freshen up' the place by giving it a lick of paint, but even before you pop the first tin of primer, Senior Spouses will be arguing more than the Pope and Michelangelo did over the Sistine Chapel. (The Pope *had* thought the ceiling was going to be Eggshell Blue, that is what was *clearly agreed upon*, but you turn your back for four years and you will be surprised what happens.)

The first argument you will have when it comes to painting is Colour Selection. Not that long ago there were only eight colours: red and yellow and pink and blue, some others we can't remember in order, and then we all could *sing a rainbow, sing a rainbow, sing rainbow too*. Many of these colours were Primary Colours, so called because they were the only colours primary school children were allowed to paint their dreadful pictures with, which we then had to stick on the fridge and lavish undeserved praise upon.

Now there are so many colours that even Purple has 32 different subcategories, and before you get even a fifth of a way down the third Paint Chart you will be envying the blind for their carefree lives. (As opposed to the colour-blind, like your Male Senior Spouse who has no sense of taste at all. This is unfair as they can taste sausages and frequently do, but you are right when it comes to interior design; your spouse may well be the tasteless love child of Elvis Presley and Liberace.)

After you have finished the different paint selections, or drafting your divorce papers (it is often neck and neck), you must show your choices to a Professional Painter. No, not an artist, one of the ones who actually earn money and rarely cut their ears off so Don McLean can write a song about them.

Painters *will* paint whatever you like, but they do have good taste, so listen carefully if they say any of the following Trigger Words about your colour choices:

'**Striking**' = clearly one of you hit the other to get their way on this one

'**Vivid**' = you will not need electric lighting, these rooms will glow in the dark

'**Bold**' = would only suit a Bowling Alley

'**Very in vogue**' = you took it from this month's *Vogue*, didn't you?

'**Adventurous**' = Indiana Jones would run in terror from this interior

'**A bit Rococo**' = you're snorting quite a bit of Cocoa, aren't you? There can be no other explanation for these choices.

Sensible Seniors will realise that life is short, and Seniors' lives even shorter, and will go with Beige. Yes, it's safe and boring, but unless we're talking about sex, these are always two good qualities for Seniors to embrace when it comes to indoor lifestyle choices. Beige it is, then. (Although Eggshell Blue would pair well with the Kitchen, after the renovation he doesn't know about yet, of course. *Hmm...*)

CHAPTER 16

Senior Moments in Poetry

SENIORS ARE THE LAST GENERATION THAT HAD POETRY BEATEN into them at school when beatings and poetry were still legally allowed. Let us review Great Poets and Poetry and see what your Senior Memories have retained.

The Rime of the Ancient Mariner: by Samuel Taylor Coleridge. (Note: Should obviously be 'Rhyme' of the Ancient Mariner but Coleridge was taking a lot of opium by this stage and had stopped paying attention to his copyeditors.)

As the Senior Student will recall, the Ancient Mariner would '*stoppeth one in three*', which was a lucky break for the other two because the poor sap who got stopped had to listen to a very long poem about an Albatross, on which the Ancient Mariner blamed all his personal problems.

This seems unfair, especially as the Ancient Mariner was the one who decided to hang the dead Albatross around his neck, which obviously would have been quite a conversation piece on a first date, but you would be unlikely to get a second one.

The moral of the poem was a) don't shoot Albatross, and b) be very wary of starting to listen to any story told to you by an Ancient Mariner. Their story is unlikely to be more exciting than *JAWS* and will not feature Robert Shaw or Richard Dreyfuss, whose performances were key to *that* story gripping you in the first place.

Coleridge also famously wrote *Xanadu*, which was a great poem and a surprise hit for Olivia Newton-John. The film was rubbish though, came out in 1980 and it did not even stoppeth one in three from going to see *The Empire Strikes Back* instead, which was a wiser choice.

Lord Byron: Byron was a *Romantic,* so romantic in fact that he fell in love with his own sister, which even Shelley agreed was a step too far. After leaving Oxford, Byron was an instant sensation, as he himself said, '*I awoke and found myself famous*'. (His publicist had obviously leaked the thing about the sister.)

Being a famous poet made Byron remarkable, as almost every other poet awakes to find themselves very unfamous. Even Philip Larkin could only get recognised in Woolworths if he was conspicuously carrying a copy of *The Whitsun Weddings*, which ate up a lot of his Saturdays. In between being heroic and fighting in wars he had not been invited to, Bryon wrote some excellent poetry, such as:

> *She walks in beauty, like the night*
> *Of cloudless climes and starry skies;*
> *And all that's best of dark and bright*
> *Meet in her aspect and her eyes;*

Even the most Bored Fifth Former will admit this is pretty good stuff, especially when you consider it was about his sister, who must have been some girl.

Byron wrote much longer verse epics like *Don Juan* and *Childe Harolde's Pilgrimage*, neither of which you have read so don't bother trying to nod sagely like you have. Byron died while fighting in the Greek War of Independence, which was odd as he was neither Greek nor Independent (he voted Tory, which was compulsory as he went to Harrow).

Bryon is also the rare poet to have become a word: '*Byronesque*', which basically means '*really cool and sexy*'. We should all be so lucky, and there is still time so pick up your quill and have a Senior Go. (Avoid writing about your sister though, keep it neutral.)

Percy Bysshe Shelley: Apart from his difficult name, which sticks for some reason, the only thing Seniors can remember about Shelley is that his wife, Mary Shelley, wrote *Frankenstein*. Worse than that, she wrote it over *one weekend* after Shelley, Byron and Mary Shelley all decided to have a writing competition, which is the sort of thing people did for fun before the internet was invented.

If Shelley was still alive today he would be really pissed at how much more famous his wife's quick creation is than his entire lifetime of work; although he would really enjoy watching *Young Frankenstein* taking the piss. (You should watch it, too. Gene Wilder, Madeline Kahn, Marty Feldman – it's fab.)

Oh, Shelley also wrote the famous poem *Ozymandias*, one of the best Ozy poems not written by Banjo Paterson. For clarity, we should point out that Shelley was no relation to Shelley Long, who did not stay long on *Cheers*, which is a shame because she was great as Diane.

The Ruby Hat of Omar Siam: This was not actually the name of this poem, but you got away with it at school if you said it quickly enough and kept a neutral expression. It contains the famous line: '*A jug of wine, a loaf of bread, and thou*' which was all the poet needed before he found out how bad carbs were. There is a lot of sugar in wine, too, but sometimes wine is needed to make thou more attractive, so it's swings and roundabouts, isn't it?

Although *The Rubaiyat of Omar Khayyam* was very beautiful and mystical and eastern and used the word '*Beloved*' a great deal, it was not, as the public was led to believe, written by Omar Khayyam the 'Astronomer-Poet of Persia'. It was written by Edward FitzGerald, a rich toff who hung around with Tennyson and Thackeray and shrewdly decided that it would be bit more commercial to, well, lie.

He was right, wrote, made a bomb out of it and bought a yacht which he cheekily named *The Scandal* and spent the rest of his life sailing about Greece having a wonderful time, with many jugs of wine and quite a few attractive thous.

As such, FitzGerald is a model for all poets, mostly a miserable indoor type who rarely go yachting. A model for Seniors too: you could go yachting if you fancied. (Well, at least buy a loaf a bread. I think giving up carbs has made thou a bit grumpy lately.)

Keats: Like all good poets Keats died tragically, young and right next to the Spanish Steps to make things easier for the tourists. Byron said that Keats was 'murdered by his critics', but tuberculosis was a more likely suspect according to the coroner. We have never heard of a critic murdering anyone in particular, although they did kill the production of *Grease on Ice* stone dead, which was particularly unfair to Olivia Newton-John who was doing her best after *Xanadu* bombed.

Keats liked Autumn, believing it to be '*a season of mists and mellow fruitfulness*'; personally, we have always thought of it as '*the season where the leaves change colour*' but we are not immortal poets. Then again, we did make it past 24, which is more than Keats did.

Keats also wrote *Ode to a Nightingale*, which was lovely but a complete waste of time as Nightingales rarely read poetry, they prefer Dick Francis novels.

Every Senior Student recalls that Keats's most famous poem was *Ode to a Grecian Urn*. Most Grecians urn very little, but they are a handsome and beautiful people and do look great on vases. Keats believed that '*a thing of beauty is a joy forever*', but he obviously would have changed this opinion if he had seen the remake of *Cats*.

Wordsworth: William Wordsworth lived in the Lake District which meant he was perpetually soggy, like so much of his verse. The man could not even *see* a field of daffodils without writing reams of rhymes about it at once, all lovingly transcribed by his sister Dorothy, who kept waiting for Bryon to turn up as he knew how to make a sister's day slightly more exciting. Anyway, the famous poem *Daffodils* is an excellent example for Seniors of Poets Getting Carried Away.

Wordsworth did not '*wander lonely as a cloud*', firstly his sister was right next to him taking notes and secondly, clouds do *not* wander, they drift. We doubt if Wordsworth knew much about the circulation movement of the average Cumulonimbus. We would not hold that against him in ordinary conversation, but this was written down and Dorothy really should have said something.

Still writing when it was important to rhyme every time, Wordsworth was not at his best when giving daffodil locations. As you will hopefully recall, as we just mentioned it, Wordsworth was pretending to be a cloud:

> *That floats on high o'er vales and hills,*
> *When all at once I saw a crowd,*
> *A host, of golden daffodils;*
> *Beside the lake, beneath the trees,*
> *Fluttering and dancing in the breeze.*

'Trees' and 'Breeze' are not what we or Byron would call Top-Drawer Rhyming. We are but inches away here from *every little breeze seems to whisper Louise, the birds in the trees*, etc. Strict Seniors will note also that Wordsworth cheats by using the word *'o'er'* instead of *over*. Poets, if you can't get the syllables to match, that is the time to crack open the thesaurus, not the time to lose a consonant for convenience. Sheer laziness.

We are o'er Wordsworth and have been since school. Bliss it was *not* to be alive and learning this guff, and to be young was very hellish when you had to recite it in front of the chalkboard.

'The Boy Stood on The Burning Deck, Whence All Around Had Fled': Bit of a nitwit, wasn't he? I mean, a deck is usually surrounded by water; if it is even smouldering *slightly* that is a pretty good indication that you should flee. Whence others flee, take the hint, sonny. Leave the 'Going Down with the Ship' heroics to the Captain, that's what he gets paid for. At least move around a bit on the Burning Deck, don't just stand there. (Honestly, you wonder how some of these boys passed the naval exam in the first place, most of them couldn't locate their own navel with the help of a map.)

Spoiler Alert: the boy did not make it. This famous line was penned by the unfamous poet Felicia Hemans from her only famous poem *Casabianca*. At the end of *Casabianca* Claude Rains orders his men to *'Round up the usual suspects'* and he and Bogie walk slowly into the fog. It was great, why Felicia did not put this in the poem is beyond us. This is why you are unfamous, Felicia. *'As Time Goes By'* alone would have made you a fortune in royalties.

Alfred Lord Tennyson: The only poet to use Lord as his middle name, he was also made a Lord, so he was Two Lords, which confused everyone, particularly W.G. Grace when he was trying to get directions to Lords.

Tennyson frequently asked girls named Maud to come into the garden. If they did come, they too would have to listen to a very long poem and would often pray for the Ancient Mariner to turn up and start talking about dead birds.

Tennyson was very popular with Queen Victoria: *'Anyone for Tennyson?'* she would famously shout as she sprang towards the court. (The Royal Court, there was no Poetry Court, as modernists refused to obey the rules and keep the verse within the lines.)

Tennyson wrote many memorable poems but the two Seniors remember are *The Lady of Shalott* and *Ulysses*. The Lady of Shalott was very glamorous but could not follow the simplest of instructions, such as Do Not Look At Camelot. You can guess what happened next, dear reader, and most of you can still recite it:

> *Out flew the web and floated wide;*
> *The mirror crack'd from side to side;*
> *'The curse is come upon me,' cried*
> *The Lady of Shalott.*

Big deal, the curse came once a month to all Female Seniors for decades, they did not go around breaking mirrors, although they were justifiably moody for a few days.

The Mirror Crack'd from Side to Side was later stolen by Agatha Christie for one of the really fun Miss Marples. Lady Shalott was not in it, but Liz Taylor was, along with Tony Curtis, Rock Hudson and Angela Lansbury. Lansbury is a model for Sensible Seniors and has never intentionally broken a mirror in her life, although she did once punch Danny Kaye after he mucked up one too many takes of 'The Vessel with the Pestle'. (He got it confused with the Chalice from the Palace.)

Rudyard Kipling: These days Kipling is regarded as 'problematic', which is code for 'huge racist', but there is no need to use code: he wrote a poem called *The White Man's Burden*, he was hardly hiding his racialist light under a bushel. On the other hand, Kipling did freely admit that Gunga Din was a better man than he was, so we shall put him down in the 'bet each way' racist column. Personal views aside, he wrote like a dream: short stories, novels, Hymns, Poems, Recessionals and *The Jungle Book*.

Neck and neck with '*The Bare Necessities*', Kipling's most well-known poem is '*If*', a rather depressingly long list of all the stuff you have to do to be a man, my son, yet somehow it manages to inspire even though you know you will never actually '*walk with Kings yet retain the common touch*'.

We have the common touch part covered, but the closest we ever got to the former was strolling briskly in proximity to Billie Jean King at the Australian Open in 1974. (We hummed '*Philadelphia Freedom*' for a little bit, but she turned and glared at us and we stopped.)

CHAPTER 17

Senior Moments at the Supermarket

As SENIORS WILL RECALL, SUPERMARKETS ARE A RELATIVELY new invention, created in the 1950's by George Reeves when he and Lois got sick of the corner store always being out of Canned Tuna and their Maltesers being stale.

Supermarkets have changed a lot since then; please note the following problem areas and advice concerning common products bought by Seniors:

Milk

Getting milk used to be a simple affair. A whistling Milkman would leave a pint in a Glass Bottle at the front gate every morning and we would zoom out the door in a desperate dash to get to it before the magpie pecked right through the alluring Red Foil Top. (This did not happen every single day, sometimes the foil was silver.) Then a battle royale would begin about *who* was going to get the cream at the top, the traditional first fight of the day before the squabbling could begin about *who* would get first dibs on the Sports Section.

There were no brands and there was only Full Cream Milk, although as mentioned above, the bottle was not *full* of cream, only the top. If it was full of cream it would have saved many arguments but then again we all would have dropped dead via heart attack by the age of 50.

Now a bewildering assortment of milks in Plastic Containers confronts the Senior at the Supermarket. The following are the main offenders, suitably explained:

Lite Milk: A ridiculous lie, weighs exactly the same, says so on the back of the container.

Skim Milk: 'Scam Milk' more like. This is a litre of water with two thimbles of milk dropped in and shaken about for ten seconds. Apparently it makes you live longer, but is it worth it if you have to drink this stuff every day?

Non-Homogenised Milk: Milk that refused to watch Rock Hudson movies. Grow up, Milk, this is the 21st century.

Farmer's Own: Milk stolen from Farmers. Happens a lot to Dairy Farmers in particular and our heart goes out to them. Surely the Police can do something about this brazen daily theft? (The Fuzz are probably being fed Skim Milk and don't have the energy.)

Home Brand Milk: Hoss and Little Joe have branded each bottle so milk rustlers will not steal it. You would think this is unnecessary but look at what happened to Farmer's Own.

Our Senior Advice is to stick to Full Cream Milk, preferably name brand, and then leave it on your own front porch and watch the magpies get their beaks bent pointlessly trying to peck through the plastic top, which is now usually blue for some reason. Immensely satisfying and nostalgic, especially if you have the Sports Section all to yourself while waiting for the fun to begin.

Bread

Again, this used to be simple. We got it from the Baker. (You could ask the Candle-Stick Maker, but he would flick wax at you and tell you to get knotted.) Mother allowed us to have Brown Bread at home and White Bread when we went out to Cafés. Now the whole thing has gotten completely out of hand. Seniors should be wary of the following:

Wonder White: The wonder is that this stuff used to be good for four days, now it goes stale as soon as the Supermarket Scanner goes *beep*. We suspect that the Bread Council gradually discovered all the preservative chemicals that worked and had them removed to give the other breads half a chance.

Multi-Grain: The wishy-washy Charlie Brown of breads. Make a decision, Bread, are you supposed to be tasty or good for us? Bitter experience has taught all Seniors you cannot be both, with the possible exception of Eartha Kitt who was certainly both for much of the 1950's. The dull fence sitter of dough, Multi-Grain makes as much sense as pouring half a glass of full cream milk and then adding skim for the rest.

Sourdough: The clue is in the name. How on earth did this baking mistake become popular? Every waitress at a café *knows* people hate it; they always say, 'We *only* have sourdough, is that all right?' with an '*I share your pain*' expression. This is like the Quiche plague all over again, every sane person secretly *hates* this stuff, but like Brioche, it is taking over our Bread Freedom by stealth. Resist and buy Non-Sourdough, you know, actual Bread.

Tip Top: Mmm. 'Round About the Middle' would be a less appealing but far more accurate name.

Helga's Traditional: Basically a large brown crust with some bread hidden in the middle. Either Helga forgets to check the oven when the pinger goes off or she is doing this on purpose. Helga should be made aware that Traditionally we all *hate* the crust. As children, we were lied to and told it made our hair grow curly. Once bitten, twice shy, Helga, and about two bites is all you shall get from us.

Rustic White: White bread that has gone rusty. Tastes suspiciously like sourdough. What have you ever known that was 'rustic' and ready to be lived in or consumed? Looks like something Worzel Gummidge produces from his pocket. No thank you.

Let us cut to the chase: Sensible Seniors should find a Nice Local Bakery, ask them no questions about the amount of sugar they use, and choose 'Brown' or 'White'. Man cannot live by bread alone; but it's pretty good if you remember to Keep it Simple, Senior.

Biscuits

For many decades, many Seniors thought they were going mad because they would *swear* that recipes of once beloved biscuits like Butternut Cookies and Iced VoVos were being *ever so slightly* changed. Nobody believed them and even heartless Senior Spouses would stare at you like Charles Boyer in *Gaslight* and tell you that you were imagining things, my dear, why don't you go upstairs and have a nice nap, etc.

But then came the Great BBQ Shapes Scandal and a humiliated Arnott's were forced to admit that they *had* changed the recipe and thought we wouldn't notice. Well we *did* and we won as Arnott's made a pathetic crawl back to what they called the Traditional Recipe but was actually just the Proper Recipe.

The cost of good biscuits is Eternal Vigilance and it is your duty as a Senior to buy a packet of Arnott's Shortbread Creams every now and again and get stuck in to make sure no funny business is going on. Oh and some Kingstons. Actually, let's get some Honey Jumbles, too, can't be too careful.

Cadbury Chocolates

Speaking of companies that try to get away with switcheroos, Seniors are keeping a vigilant watch on Cadbury. When Professor Julius Sumner Miller was alive we could be sure that there was a glass and a half of full cream dairy milk in every bar of Cadbury's chocolate. Then for some unexplained reason, the good Professor would try to stick a boiled egg inside a milk bottle with the aid of a candle. (What he then did with the egg or the candle was not explained, and we are sure many questions were asked when that bottle was sent back to the milkworks.)

Anyway, the point is this: there is *no more silver tinfoil wrapping* around Cadbury's chocolate. Why? And if they have changed this, *what else are they changing*? We realise that Cadbury is obviously very busy being a butler to Richie Rich, but we would appreciate some answers.

Spices

Salt and Pepper are spices. That, along with Curry Powder for the daredevils, was enough for everyone until about 1986 when suddenly the spice section of the Supermarket exploded endlessly like some culinary version of *Arabian Nights*.

They started sensibly enough with '*Chilli Flakes*' and '*Oregano*' but a new spice was added every day, leading to small bottles called '*Moroccan Mix*' and '*Tuscan Lemon*' that seemed like a good idea at the time, have clearly been used *once and once only*, and now clog your Senior Spice Rack for eternity.

There are mores spices available in the average Woollies than you can possibly count. In fact, they have given up on Alphabetical and are now using the Dewey Decimal System to try to sort them. Who buys all this stuff? *'Nashville Style Spicy Chicken Seasoning'*? Is Conway Twitty coming to dinner?

Admit it, you are still not entirely sure what Tumeric is, even at this stage. Seniors are advised to stick to Salt and Pepper, keep your old spices as a memento mori not to buy at whim, and splash out on *'Rock Salt'* if you ever want to – pardon the pun – spice it up a little again. (Male Seniors are also advised to use *'Old Spice'*; it is getting a little whiffy on non-bath days. Yes, we have noticed.)

Meat Specials

Not special at all, that's why nobody has bought it and it is now marked down at a reduced price. Unfortunately, Seniors who buy Meat Specials are always overcome by an irresistible urge to tell whomever they serve the meat to what a *great bargain* they got, resulting in a long thoughtful stare from the dinee as they suddenly realise precisely how much, or rather how little, their spouse/host values them.

Avoid the Meat Special, even if you are doing a stew, you *know* you will still sniff it suspiciously and add extra pepper to be sure. Is this how you wish to live the remainder of your Senior life? As a Meat Sniffer? We hope not. Pony up and buy meat that tastes less like a pony.

Shampoo and Conditioner

Once upon a time there was *only* shampoo and our hair was left to condition itself, which it usually managed quite well as long as we whacked in a bit of Brylcreem or Hairspray, depending on your sex and how much sex you wanted.

Then along came 'Conditioner' and suddenly we were all required to remain stationary in the shower for three minutes as we waited for the conditioner to do its magic. (It wasn't compulsory to remain stationary; a free-flowing dance was allowed as long as your head avoided being hit by water, but dancing in the shower is not advised for any Senior who hopes to make it back to the bathmat with all limbs and both hips intact.)

To compete with Conditioner, Shampoos decided to become increasingly specialised and complicated and now Seniors are obliged to make difficult value judgements about whether our hair is *Normal*, *Extra-Dry*, in need of *Moisture Repair*, *Nutri-Repair*, *Colour Therapy*, *Blooming*, or perhaps we have *Problem Hair* that is in need of *Addictive Brilliant Shine*. (Is the *Brilliant Shine* really *that* addictive? Is there a 12-Step Program just to get back to *Extra-Dry*?)

Time Sensitive Seniors (and really there are no other kinds) are advised to give up and buy Decore. It's as good as any other and had that nice ad where everybody sang along to '*Duke of Earl*', which at least is fun.

Soap

What kind of soap you buy says a lot about the type of Senior you are, which can be embarrassing when other nosy shoppers are watching our purchase: Imperial Leather? *Interesting. Not a fan of democracy when it comes to soap, bit of Franco in the bathtub, are we?* Botanical Lemon Grass? *Well, la de dah, Mr Joseph Banks, enjoy your scrub.* Palmolive Gold Daily Deodorant? *My God, just how smelly are you?*

We would advise Seniors of Means to purchase Pears. It is the soap used by the Queen, By Royal Warrant, even says so on the wrapper. (We were unaware the Queen even had a warrant out on her; presumably the papers had the taste and discretion to hush it up. Was she shoplifting Pears and this is the arrangement they have worked out? It is not out of the question, Pears is quite expensive and we bet Prince Philip watches her weekly household budget like a hawk.)

Pears is a lovely soap, although we do end up thinking about the Queen a lot when we are bathing. This could be embarrassing when we were younger but is oddly comforting as the years tick by. Republicans should obviously feel free to choose a different soap but probably not Imperial Leather, for similar reasons.

Toothbrushes

Another needlessly problematic purchase area for all Seniors. Our grandparents never had this trouble, they all had Dentures and just had to pop them in a glass of fizzy water every night. Seniors today have usually retained their teeth and once again are trapped in an endless agony of choice.

Hard, Medium or Soft used to be states we hoped to control in the bedroom, now it is but the preliminary step in selecting the curved triple-grip crown-embracing ripple-bristle device that apparently is the bare minimum for any toothbrush.

Take this Senior Tip: next time you are at the rather-too-super-market, look hard and buy a small 'Travel Kit' in the toiletries section. Inside you will be overjoyed to find a small replica of what we all used to recognise as a Standard Toothbrush. Yes, you will feel a bit *Land of the Giants* when you use it, but this is a small price to pay for the nostalgia of using something that still looks the way it should as you polish your pearly whites in the night. (And morning, don't be lazy.)

CHAPTER 18

Senior Moments in Theatre

Senior Theatrical Warnings for the Senior Punter

As a discerning Senior Patron of Theatre, we do hope you spend your dosh wisely by purchasing a ticket to a performance of *Senior Moments*, the hilarious comedy revue, inevitably coming soon and very reasonably priced to a Theatre Near You. But beware: other productions will try to trick the Careless Senior into attending shows that *seem* suitable but contain no actual enjoyment whatsoever. (Non-enjoyment is actually a pre-condition of Arts Funding in several States and at least one Territory.)

The Savvy Senior is advised to avoid the following types of plays:

Plays That Involve a 'Difficult Choice': This means that it's a play about euthanasia, but they don't want you to realise that before you're halfway through Act One and it's too late for a refund. Puff quote from Andrew Denton on the billboard is one of the prime warning signs.

'An Evening with…': One-Man Plays used to be enough to satisfy even the most egomaniacal of performers; but now they have been replaced by a new threat: *'An evening with…'* Essentially an excuse for the lazier Senior Thespian to perform 'highlights' from the bits of their old plays they can still half-remember, interspersed with a few choice self-serving anecdotes about their 'journey'. Triple red alarm if 'Q&A' is billed as part of the evening. Oh, so now we're supposed to be part of the show? Fine, let's get a percentage of the door as well. No? Didn't think so.

Plays That Are 'Ripped from Today's Headlines': Oh dear. This means that the playwright read a newspaper (usually *The Guardian*) eight months ago and now you are watching a hastily written first draft that should have been slowly rewritten about some issue that seemed temporarily important last Autumn. At least when you read a newspaper there's a crossword to do when you get bored.

Shakespearian Plays That Feature 'Gender-Blind Casting': Works wonderfully if the audience is also blind, although they will spend most of the performance wondering why Othello is a soprano. The Elizabethans used 'gender-blind casting', too; all the parts were played by men. Watch it, luvvies.

Plays with 'Real Dialogue from Real People': This used to be known as eavesdropping, now apparently it is 'Art'. Yes, the tedious conversations you carefully avoided listening to at the bus stop are now being repeated to you word-for-word by actors wearing giant headphones. Sheer cheek. This is one of the two signs that a playwright is really losing it. The other being…

Plays That Spring from 'Fascinating Research': Playwrights are supposed to make it up, not look it up. But these days everything from dull 19th-century Royal Commission transcripts, long-lost family letters that have been tragically found, and of course, the inevitable war diaries are all being reheated and served up to powerless patrons in full first-person horror. There are now only two diaries left from World War One that have not been turned into a play, and one of them is by the Kaiser. The other consists solely of recorded rainfall at the Somme during August 1917 and is being turned into a solemn two-hander at the Belvoir entitled *Wet Before Dawn*. Avoid.

Plays Where Actors Pretend to Be Children: Actors love this sort of thing, audiences do not. Other people's children are seldom tolerable, other people pretending to be children never are. High-pitched voices, high-waisted pants, lisps galore and faux innocent dialogue like *'daddy no come home last night; mummy cwyed and dwank a whole bottle of mummy juice'* await.

We don't blame mummy one bit and in fact are two steps ahead of her. 'Suffer the little children,' said the Lord. 'But I'll need a pretty stiff gin to make it through this rubbish' (Lord Olivier, not the one from Nazareth).

Plays That Have Been Translated: The French are superb at many things, like cooking, pulling off extra-marital affairs and surrendering. But adapting their plays into English is not one of their strengths. Quite frankly, we think they can't be bothered to do it properly and expect us to learn French instead. We *did* learn French at school for a year, but unless the play revolves exclusively around the pen of my aunt being lost in the garden of my uncle, we shall be lost.

The Gallic Non-Enjoyment Rule applies to French works from any century. English people have been politely trying to find Molière funny since 1658; it is time to give up the struggle, just like the French would in an important war.

As for the Russians, it's been over a century now and nobody can decide whether Chekhov is supposed to be tragic or comic.

Be honest, the only Chekov you actually look forward to seeing is the one who used to sit next to Mr Sulu in *Star Trek*.

Plays That Are a 'Neglected Masterpiece': Unlike animals, plays are usually neglected for excellent reasons such as boredom and the fact that nobody went to see the damn thing in the first place. 'Forgotten Treasure' is another phrase to be careful of. Believe you me, we know what Producers are like and if the play produced any actual treasure it would still be running on the RSL circuit right now.

Neglected Masterpieces are invariably selected by Neglected Artistic Directors of theatre companies who are sick of putting on '*The Odd Couple*' and want to get some attention by reviving Neil Simon's neglected masterpiece '*The Star-Spangled Girl*'. Don't.

Plays That Are an Allegory: If it's an allegory, it's got no story. And no, don't say *Animal Farm*, that was a book first. Those animals were rotten farmers anyway, didn't understand the first thing about crop rotation. Four Legs Good, Third Act Dreadful.

Many worthy but miserable productions will try to hoodwink Seniors into attending by using secret theatrical code. Keep a sharp lookout for the following words in theatrical ads or reviews and use our Senior Theatrical Translator to work out what they actually mean.

Senior Theatrical Translator for Suspicious Words and Phrases:

'**Challenging**' = *Dreadful*

'**Confronting**' = *Leave before interval*

'**An incredible re-imagining**' = *You cannot imagine what this nitwit has done to a once-good play*

'**An inspired production**' = *Director clearly on drugs*

'**Mesmerising**' = *Critic fell asleep*

'**Haunting**' = *Critic had nightmare while asleep*

'**A very brave performance**' = *Actor takes togs off at age when they probably shouldn't*

Also watch out for the following red alarm words: '*daring*', '*bold*', '*visionary*' and especially the phrases '*uncomfortable truths*' or '*harsh truths*'. (If we wanted a lecture, dear, we'd go back to uni.)

Special Warning: if the director is described as an '*enfanté terriblé*', the production will just be 'terriblé'. Oh, and be very careful if the show stars someone really famous from overseas who could be getting a lot more money for a movie. They only want to do miserable things to prove that they're artists. Watch out! (Maggie Smith is the exception; she is just in it for the dosh.)

Things, Subjects and Playwrights to Avoid

Any play where people are 'searching' for things: Whether it's children, lost pearls, innocence, childhood, or, 90% of the time, 'the truth'. Trust us, you will be searching for the bar at interval and won't come back.

Shakespearean plays you have never heard of: There is a reason that you have never seen *King Henry VIII Part 2*. Or 'the rarely performed *Pericles*'. It's like a rarely heard Beatles song. It means it's not very good.

Nation-Portraying Dance 'Celebrations' that feature more people on stage than there are seats in the theatre. Yes, the 1,000 dancers in the poster may well showcase '900 years of Tibetan history in 90 minutes' but you'd be better off on the couch watching Gene Kelly dancing on his own with an umbrella.

Eugene O'Neill: He wasn't kidding when he called the thing *Long Day's Journey into Night*, it will be 3 am before you get home and you still won't know what's happened.

Any play that says it stars Googie Withers: Googie left us in 2011, but some unscrupulous producers still try it on; a surprisingly successful trick, as we found out five years ago in the first season of *Senior Moments*, starring Googie Withers.

Harold Pinter: It's been 60 years, can we just say he's a genius, admit that no one enjoys it and move on? His best play is *The Caretaker*, for goodness sake. If you want to spend two hours listening to a tramp mumble and make increasingly sinister threats, go to your city's train terminus any night and get that for free.

Shakespearean comedies: Apart from *Much Ado About Nothing*, *A Midsummer Night's Dream* and *As You Like It*. Look, the guy wrote timeless dramas, but you pretending that you understand 450-year-old Elizabethan puns about pomegranates and shoemaking is a complete waste of time. 'By my thumb I strike it, and so it justly falls. Not tupping, but by mine hand, sir!' etc. *No one understands this!* Give it up.

Ibsen: Honestly, can you even name a character?

Safe Playwrights for Seniors

George Bernard Shaw, Alan Bennett, Neil Simon, David Williamson, Noel Coward, Terence Rattigan, Oscar Wilde, Alan Ayckbourn and Tom Stoppard unless he is writing another damn play about maths. (We get it, Tom, you can do long division and explain what an integer is, we're all very impressed. Get back to writing about minor characters in Hamlet, that was top stuff.)

Playwright Use-By Dates

Just like milk and Elizabeth Taylor's husbands, some things inevitably go off and have to be disposed of after a brief period of enjoyment. The same rule applies to once safely entertaining Playwrights. Whether the cause is breaking up with Marilyn Monroe or getting blotto one too many times with Norman Mailer, sometimes even the great ones totally lose it.

Senior Patrons should observe the following use-by dates:

Arthur Miller: 1964.

Edward Albee: 1973. (And that's being kind. Anything after Act 2 in *Who's Afraid of Virginia Woolf?* if we're being bitchy.)

Tennessee Williams: 1968 or whenever he wrote that play about the lizard.

Steven Berkoff: From birth onwards. (Honestly, critics and audiences are both just frightened to death of that man. Looked like he was going to attack you at any moment, even if you were in the balcony. He's two oceans away and we're still worried about putting this in the book.)

CHAPTER 19

Senior Moments at Family Occasions

As Seniors grow older, the more Family Occasions they will be required to attend. The following guide should be observed for smooth sailing and leaving without having disgraced yourself. (Of course, if you would like to disgrace yourself, we have a few good ideas on that, too. Pay attention and read on.)

Grandchild Occasions

Art Shows: We can't believe it either, but now children, *actual children*, are given '*showcases*' and '*exhibitions*' at many schools. As Grand Seniors, we are graciously invited to attend when we would rather be watching repeats of *The Man from U.N.C.L.E.*, which we have just found on *Splash!* or whatever the name of the new free channel is.

Here is the kicker: after wandering around with a glass of paint stripper and a Jatz Cracker with cheddar on top for 15 minutes, having now suitably patronised (in both senses of the word) the '*exhibition*' of our grandchild's class, we are then expected to buy at least one of these offerings! *With real money!*

In the old days, this is the sort of scam we would expect from Basquiat or Andy Warhol, but at least one of those two could draw and Andy could colour in a Soup Can like nobody's business.

If schools want the children to get a *real* taste of what it is like to be an Artist, have five people turn up to the exhibition, two of them asking '*if they can just use the loo*', and the others leaving without making eye contact or buying *anything*. Then the school can send the Young Artists a staggeringly large bill for 'staging costs and promotion' and little Betty or Bobby shall realise that a career in accountancy might be a wiser choice. It usually is.

School Concerts: Yes, yes, we know *your* grandchild is wonderful – the next Mozart or Barbra Streisand – but I think we can all agree that the other children are hacks and a waste of our Senior Time and attention.

Unfortunately, School Concert Organisers are no fools; apart from whatever number your grandchild will bless with their presence, there is always a Group Finale, which ensures you can't sneak out as soon the bit you are interested in is done, and you have to wait the full four hours. Honestly, it's like an EST meeting in there, except the only moment of self-revelation you have is that you can't *stand* watching children play *Twinkle, Twinkle, Little Star* on massed violins.

We suggest the following strategy: when your Grandchild has finished the '*Dance of the Sugar Plum Fairy*' or a powerful reading of *Clancy of the Overflow*, simply stare at your mobile phone aghast for a split second, then say, 'My God, not *Rog*!' No more, no less. Then, using acting skills that all of those children who just murdered *Toad of Toad Hall* should learn from, leave *as conspicuously as possible*.

The Foolish Senior will try to *sneak* out of a concert, thus looking *sneaky*. You, on the other hand are clearly and openly in crisis. Like the Red Sea, squeaky school chairs shall part for you and you will have the sympathy of all as you mournfully depart the Assembly Hall.

You will be home in time to watch Napoleon Solo karate chop his last Russian and none shall be the wiser. Yes, you *will* miss the Group Finale, but this is usually an ensemble off-key rendition of '*The Rainbow Connection*', of which your Grandchild will be just a tiny coloured dot, like the way crowd members used to look at the Moscow Olympics before they turned the pictures over and you realised they were a Giant Bear With A Hat On.

In any case, the School Concert will be recorded by a thousand mobile phones, filmed from a multiplicity of angles that a U2 Concert Video could only have dreamt of in the 1980's; watch it later at leisure, Post-*U.N.C.L.E.*

Birthday Parties: Not that we shall harp on it, but back in the day you got a cake, a dozen school chums at most and a game of Pin the Tail on the Donkey, then it was time for Sweetie Bags and your party was over.

(All right, once in while you would get an Aged Magician who would trap one of your more attractive Aunts in some Silver Rings and occasionally there was a Punch and Judy Showman. When was the last time you even *saw* a Punch and Judy Show? They were such fun. Unfortunately, as Seniors will recall, the plot of every show revolved around Mr Punch and Mrs Punch hitting each other repeatedly with sticks and then Mr Punch would try to *kill the baby* – sounds bad, was hilarious – by dropping it out the window. It was un-P.C. even in Shakespeare's time and it was a miracle it lasted as long as it did.)

Anyway, we have strayed from our Senior Central Point, which is that *our* birthday parties were generally sparse affairs that Oliver Cromwell would approve of, as opposed to the crazed bacchanal and carnivale combined that the Children's Birthday Party Industrial Complex has become today.

If it is held 'at home', you will be stunned to watch a sort of Wiggles version of a P.E. Class going on, with the children voluntarily participating in the kind of workout they used to give Marines on the obstacle course in basic training, all to the blaring soundtrack of whatever the loudest and more repetitive Taylor Swift hits of the day may be.

Then the Karaoke Machine shall begin, followed by the Jumping Castle, a Chocolate Fountain and a cameo appearance by Iron Man, Thor or Wonder Woman, taste and price dependant. (These are clearly not the *real* Thor or Wonder Woman, although one never knows if it could be Robert Downey Jr. inside the Iron Man suit; he did stranger things than that in the '90s when he was having substance issues. Who knows when the flashbacks kick in?)

Now it is time for Big Screen *Fortnite*, Pony Rides, and the consumption of a Cake for a child in single digits which is double the size of the one at your Wedding, which in its entirety *must* have cost less than this shindig. Oh, and if you are wondering when Pass the Parcel begins, stop wondering: your grandchild is too busy trying to murder a peer from Utah online in *Fortnite* to even look up, let alone deign to unwrap anything, including the 500 presents currently crushing the Hall Entry Table.

Then the children are presented with a suite of parting gifts, like Cleopatra exiting Rome on non-official business. (Presumably the Sweetie Bag is hidden in one of them, they are so big that D.B. Cooper could be hiding out in there.)

If you question any of this madness, your children will patronisingly explain that it is part of the 'Party Circuit' and the tots and their parents expect nothing less at least twice a weekend. How any of the parents avoid bankruptcy or any of the children avoid diabetes is beyond us.

Oh well, at least they still sing 'Happy Birthday' and cut the cake, so some things never change, including the temper tantrum when your grandchild only manages to blow two candles out and their more unkind 'friends' laugh.

The alternative to the home orgy is even worse: it is called TimeZone, which is appropriate as each facility is large enough to be granted its own time zone and, like a casino, it is full of flashing lights, loud computer-type noises and depressed adults and you will lose all sense of time and quite a lot of money while you are trapped in there.

Christenings: First of all, be grateful that you get a Christening, not just a Name Announcement Email. Secondly, do not obsess about making the poor infant wear the same ghastly yellowed Christening Gown that your Great-Great-Grandmother did. You are making the baby look like a Mini Miss Havisham and you should just go to Peter Alexander and buy something white.

As to Christening Nomenclature, Seniors have given up on the hope of their grandchildren having sensible first names; you will have to accept them being named after a Crayon, a type of Weather or an Element, that is Modern Life. The smart money is on the *middle* name; this is where Grandparent Battle will commence, as both matching sets try to ensure some sense of immortality by jamming a Family Name in there.

Hopefully, your own mother had a nice first name like Alice or an interesting maiden name like Vanderbilt; if she didn't, *make up one* that sounds cool and pitch it as best you can. If the Rival Grandparents succeed by placing one of *their* pedestrian family names onto *your* Grandchild's birth certificate, make sure you give them a particularly meaningful stare during that bit of the Christening where the parents recite that they shall '*promise to renounce the works of the Devil*'. If burdening a baby with the middle name 'Agnetha' is not one of the works of the Devil, then frankly I don't know what is.

Senior Occasions

There are three of these: the Big Birthday, the Big Anniversary and, God help you, the Re-Commitment Ceremony.

1. The Big Birthday: Either you have turned 70 or your child has turned 40. It's depressing either way, isn't it? Where did the time go? It wasn't spent on dutifully applying wrinkle cream if Mr Mirror is to be believed. Look, there are some perpetually perky souls who enjoy hitting the Big O's, but unless the Big O in question is Roy Orbison we are not amongst them. (We do not mean we would strike Roy Orbison, he had a tragic life as it was and sang like an Angel. And he died at 52! Natural causes too, bloody hell.)

Anyway, if it's your party do try to stay upbeat, now is not the time to be maudlin. Save that for when the guests leave, a third of the cake is still there, and you put on Peggy Lee singing '*Is That All There Is?*'

Come on, buck up! Paul McCartney is 78! Ann-Margret is 79! Bob Dylan is about to hit 80 and Harry Belafonte is still hitting it at 90! Put on '*Man Smart (Woman Smarter)*' and dance like you still have both original hips.

2. The Big Anniversary: Tread carefully here, Male Seniors. Despite your Bride's persistent protestations that she 'does not want anything big', she does. Go to Town, Paint it Red and then walk to Tiffany's and buy something sparkly if you wish your wife to retain her spark instead of retaining a Divorce Lawyer.

At bare minimum, take the immediate family to the Most Expensive Restaurant in Town; at minor maximum, contact everyone you have ever met and consider booking Luna Park. No, we are not joking, do you know how difficult it has been to remain married to you? Well, your wife does, so play it safe and max out the credit card or Option 3 *will* take place.

3. The Re-Commitment Ceremony: This used to only happen on American Sitcoms and Soaps when they had run out of every conceivable plot, but now Wedding Planners must be the ones plotting, because the Re-Commitment Ceremony has become a real thing and a real danger to all Male Seniors.

'*Oh, it will never happen to me,*' you think. Really? Here's how it happens. You have just attended a Re-Commitment Ceremony for two old friends who you thought would know better. A *strange silence* descends upon the car on your way home.

You: Poor old Harry.

Wife: What?

You: I wonder what he did to deserve that? Got caught stepping out, I suppose.

Wife: *(near tears)* I wonder what Rhonda did to *deserve* a husband that *still loved her* and was man enough to say so *in public*!

You: You should hear what he says in private. Last week we were on the 8th tee and...

Wife: Stop the car.

You: What?

Wife opens door and jumps out, shoulder rolls to halt and calls Divorce Lawyer to 'discuss options'.

All right, the shoulder roll bit rarely happens but sometimes it is a damn close thing. Soon enough you will be begging forgiveness, you were only *joking*, yes it was a *beautiful* ceremony, *very* touching and... and *yes*, why don't *we* have one?

See? Not so funny now, is it, as you stand there re-enacting your own wedding, shoes still a *bit* too tight. As is your original 'Best Man' who is already supressing snickers at the humiliation you are about to endure and rehearsing quips he shall make to his wife about the foolishness of Re-Commitment Ceremonies on the way home. Little does he know that a *strange silence* is about to descend...

CHAPTER 20

Senior Moments in Pop Music

WE ARE NOT GOING TO TALK ABOUT MODERN POP MUSIC obviously, that is all dreadful having lost its way around the same time Michael Jackson lost his original skin colour. Many young people think, if they think at all, that Senior Pop Music began and ended with The Beatles, but there was a fair amount of music being produced before the Fab Four came along and introduced the idea of being great to pop music. Before then, you could get away with almost any old rubbish, as we shall see. Here are some pop icons, songs and devices now only remembered by Seniors.

Songs about Clothes: There were a lot of these. 'A White Sport Coat (and a Pink Carnation)' was one of them. Sung by Marty Robbins, who usually sang great songs about gunfighters who were out in the west to the north of El Paso, this lugubrious ballad represented both a change of pace and a change of wardrobe for Marty. We don't imagine many gunfighters would have lasted terribly long in the Old West if they ventured out onto the streets wearing a pink carnation, let alone the obvious camouflage problems that a white sport coat would present.

As Seniors will recall, Marty sang at great length in three or four not terribly great verses about getting dressed in a White Sport Coat, then adding a Pink Carnation because he was 'all *dressed up for the dance*'. Yes, that's right, Shabby Young People, Seniors did go to some sartorial trouble even for high-school shindigs.

In case any Young People *are* reading this, a Sport Coat was a jacket that was a different colour to our black or navy pants. The Sport Coat was seldom used in a sporting context, unless you count running down the high-school hallways at great speed because we had made an unwise pass at Peggy Sue, and her angry boyfriend, usually named Johnny, was chasing us.

Another surprisingly popular song that all Seniors will be able to recite on their death beds was simply called '*Pink Shoelaces*', sung by Dodie Stevens. You see, Dodie had a guy and his name was Dooley (unusual, but presumably necessary for the rhyme scheme). He was *her* guy and she loved him truly. (We did not doubt her faithfulness, but the fact that she brought it up makes you think.) Although not good looking, heaven knows, Dodie was *wild* about his *crazy* clothes. The clothes consisted of an obsessively comprehensive list of tastelessness, namely: tan shoes with pink shoelaces, a polka dot vest and a big Panama with a purple hat band.

Dooley's other wardrobe was not specified and although unconventional, we doubt that his fashion choices alone met the clinical definition of crazy. As the song went on though, Dooley's behaviour did raise eyebrows as he took Dodie '*deep sea fishing in a submarine*' (logically impossible) and to '*drive-in movies in a limousine*' (eccentric perhaps, but still not enough to get Dooley in a rubber room for good). The cheerful and very catchy song took a surprisingly serious turn in the second half. Dooley, of his own volition, enlisted in the fighting corps (he '*had a feeling that we were going to war*'). As it turns out, Dooley was right: the Vietnam War started just a few years later but Dooley did not live long enough to see it.

Suffering from an unspecified illness in the song, Trooper Dooley insisted on immediately having his will drawn up, which consisted entirely of specifying the clothes he would wear at his impending funeral. We are sure you can guess what they were: '*they were tan shoes with pink shoelaces*', etc.

Despite the fact that her boyfriend had just died, Dodie Smith still sounded happier than Alvin and the Chipmunks on lithium and perhaps she was the one who should have been seeing a psychiatrist. If young people don't quite understand why Lennon and McCartney and Bob Dylan are still viewed as Gods by all Seniors, one listen to this song will make them realise what we lived through before their blessed arrival.

Oh, there are was also a song about an *Itsy Bitsy Teenie Weenie Yellow Polkadot Bikini*, which started off as only mildly suggestive and then became positively X-rated when an unfortunately timed wave removed the Bikini altogether and the young semi-naked lady was now left trapped out at sea. (This was in a time when being topless was still frowned upon, including in the marital bedroom for Anglicans.)

The song was left strangely unresolved; presumably the young woman drowned to preserve her modesty, a shame but a lesson to us all when selecting sexy but unsturdy beachwear. Thongs are for your feet, we have no wish to see your bottom, thank you, Young Show-Offs.

Songs about Dogs: Usually they were sad and ended up with Fido getting a bullet in the face, as in '*Old Shep*' sung by Elvis the Pelvis. (There was a reason, usually they got rabies, although in the '70s Elvis did start shooting Televisions when they annoyed him for any reason. Why he slaughtered so many innocent TV sets and yet let Colonel Tom Parker run free was one of the *many* mysteries of Elvis, but The King must have had his reasons.)

Far worse that the miserable songs about canines were the cutesy ones, and there was none cuter than *'How Much Is That Doggie in the Window?'* by Patti Page. This simple enquiry about the price of a pet dragged out for three minutes and was, believe it or not, the number one record on Billboard for 18 weeks in 1953 and sold three million copies. It was so popular that a competing cover version was also in the Top Ten *at the same time,* a sadistic torture that we cannot recall having been repeated and was subsequently banned under The Geneva Convention.

For those who are wondering, the song consisted entirely of Patti asking how much the doggie was in the window, specifying it was the one with the waggily nose, and then revealing she wanted the dog, ironically, because her boyfriend was a pussy and was afraid of burglars. After this was made unnecessarily clear, a couple of verses of futility were entered into as Patti specified the animals she did *not* want.

She did *not* want a bunny or a kitty, she was *not* keen on a parrot that talks, Patti did *not* want a *'bowl of little fishies'* as her cowardly lover *'can't take a goldfish for a walk'.* Then Elvis turned up and shot the doggie so this song could be over. Seriously, this song was so winsome and twee it may have single-handedly created Rock 'n' Roll, which may give Patti Page her sole argument for not burning in Hades for releasing this maddening twaddle.

Songs about Inanimate Objects: These were legion. Red Rubber Balls, Chewing Gum that Lost Its Flavour on The Bedpost Overnight and the anthropomorphic hit *'You're a Pink Toothbrush'* all spent time on the charts and still spend time on Senior Minds despite our best efforts to forget them. Max Bygraves sang *'You're a Pink Toothbrush',* an extremely strange song about a psychotic small boy who imagines that he overhears his parents' toothbrushes planning to marry. It was not exactly a Romance For The Ages, the woo pitching of the Male Toothbrush remained dully observational. Procedurally, it went roughly like this:

You are a Pink Toothbrush, I am a Blue Toothbrush. He then recalled they met by the Bathroom Door. The Blue Toothbrush then proposed marriage '*in haste*', with the enticing promise that they could then '*both use the same toothpaste*'. We have come a long way when it comes to Marriage Equality, but Toothbrush Nuptials are still way down the list and probably should remain there if the sole reason for matrimony is a desire to share the same tube of Colgate. By the by, the Pink Toothbrush said nothing throughout the whole song and we are guessing hated the Blue Toothbrush just as much as we did.

Johnnie Ray: Despite wearing a hearing aid and dressing more like a Methodist minister than a pop singer, Johnnie Ray was Elvis before Elvis, a pre-Rock teen sensation who prompted screams from huge crowds of shrieking, hysterical teenage girls. None were more hysterical than Johnnie, who seemed to undergo a complete nervous breakdown every time he sat down at the piano, including convulsions that would be the envy of any decent Exorcist.

'*Cry*' was his biggest hit, and cry Johnnie did as he wept, rolled and smashed himself about the soon sodden piano, exhorting the listener to overcome heartbreak by crying their eyes out like Johnnie did as soon as he even saw a Steinway. Johnnie followed that number one smash with another, also about crying, called '*The Little White Cloud That Cried*'. (The Cloud was not really crying, it was raining, but nobody had the heart to break it to Johnnie who was already weeping as it was.)

Nobody under 50 has any idea who Johnnie Ray was but he was so popular that he was shoe-horned into the film *There's*

No Business Like Show Business playing Marilyn Monroe's lover; an enviable role that made even Johnnie stop bawling for five minutes. He never made another film again for the simple reason that he decided he couldn't act, a moment of clarity that we wish came to more musical would-be thespians that we are too kind to name (i.e. the someone who rhymes with 'Bladonna' and sang '*Like a Virgin*').

The press loved Johnnie Ray and many happy hours were spent giving him nicknames like '*The Nabob of Sob*' and '*The Prince of Wails*'. Then Elvis turned up and Johnnie, like every other pop star except Frank Sinatra, began the slow fade into Obscurity. Obscurity tried to slowly fade Frank Sinatra, but Frank got Jilly and the boys to threaten to break Obscurity's legs and so The Chairman of the Board remained famous forever.

Nobel Laureate Bob Dylan was asked a few years ago what the most exciting moment in his life was and after a long pause, he replied that once, in the 1970's, he was in a lift with Johnnie Ray. Dylan was 100% serious and we are 100% sure that Johnnie Ray had absolutely no idea who Bob Dylan was or could care less.

Seniors still have a soft spot for Johnnie Ray; he was a uniquely demented performer and still makes the Senior feel better about the humiliation of having to wear a hearing aid. Johnnie Ray made it look cool, we can too. Or we can cry. Either way he is a Senior Role Model.

Novelty Songs: Novelty Songs do not exist anymore and for good reason, but they grew like topsy before the Mop Tops turned up and shut them down. '*The Monster Mash*', '*My Friend the Witch Doctor*' and '*Alley Oop*' were all massive hits and were respectively about Monsters, a Witch Doctor and a Caveman, thus departing significantly from the traditional '*I'm in Love/ We are In Love/You Dumped Me*' format that had until this time constituted popular music.

Sometimes novelty songs could be incredibly specific, such as *'Kookie, Kookie (Lend Me Your Comb)'*, which was a boppy request to borrow the hairstyling implement of Edd 'Kookie' Byrnes who, along with his greasy comb-requiring locks, appeared each week on *77 Sunset Strip* as an exceptionally hip valet who combed his hair a great deal, hence the song.

Confusingly, Kookie sang the song in duet with Connie Stevens, who played 'Cricket' Blake on *Hawaiian Eye*. (She did not play Cricket in real life, and got confused if you asked her even the most basic question about leg-spin bowling.) Connie, one would think, had plenty of combs of her own and even if Kookie lent her his comb, flying the comb back and forth from Hawaii to L.A. would have been extremely expensive.

The lyrics were not exactly a triumph, involving couplets like *'I've got smog in my noggin/ever since you made the scene'*, which did not technically rhyme, just as Edd did not technically sing, adopting more of a Rex Harrison speak-sing approach for further masterful lines like *'What's with this comb caper baby?/Why do you want to latch onto my comb?'* This thing sold a million copies.

Kookie was later parodied as the character Fonzie on *Happy Days*, but Henry Winkler resisted the temptation to sing about his own comb-lending policies, although as he and Connie Stevens are both still going strong, there is still time.

CHAPTER 21

Senior Moments in Gardening

As you become more Senior you may find yourself with an overwhelming desire to begin gardening. Do not worry, it has gripped many other former groovers in the past. For instance, George Harrison became so obsessed with gardening after he left The Beatles that he often forgot to record albums for years at a time, and when he did there were more songs about choosing the right potting mixture than his Record Company would have liked.

It's easy to become lost in the world of Gardening, particularly if you have grown a Maze. If you *are* stuck in a Maze, remember to turn left at every opportunity and always move away from the sound of the Minotaur. (The Minotaur usually turns out to be the Leaf Blower that fool next door insists on using *every* Sunday, but best to be on the Senior Safe Side.)

A Gardening Senior should be familiar with the following terms:

Perennial: This is a plant or flower that refuses to follow instructions throughout the entire year.

Annual: A plant that disappoints only once a year, i.e.:

Helpful Neighbour: Gosh, I thought your Roses would be in bloom by now, it's the *middle of spring*!

You: Why don't you stick that Leaf Blower down your pants and do us both a favour? *(You don't always say this last bit, but you do think it.)*

Annuals have been disappointing many Seniors since childhood, for instance, *CHUMS*. This Annual was at least 900 pages long but never seemed to have a decent short story in it. A suspiciously large number of the short stories had '*To Be Continued on Page 117*' at their conclusion. Page 117 was often a full-page feature on '*A Day in the Life of Len Hutton*', which rarely provided a satisfactory conclusion; a fact that even Mrs Hutton would attest to after a Hot Toddy or two.

The Greyfriars Christmas Annual was usually a bit better but *The Rupert Annual* was not. (Seniors will remember when 'Rupert' was a friendly bear who dressed in tweed and had many Adventures in the Sky etc. These days Rupert controls most of the world's media, but we do not believe it is the same bear, although Bill Badger did edit *The Sun* for a brief time in the mid-1970's.)

Evergreen: What the lawn isn't. We have strong memories that grass used to *always* be green in our childhood, and no, we are not looking through rose-coloured glasses, because then the grass would have looked pink. The amount of trouble you have to go to get your lawn not looking like Henry Fonda is just about to drive through it with the rest of the miserable cast of *The Grapes of Wrath* is unbelievable. Most lawns soak up more liquid than Richard Burton let loose in a distillery but with no discernible effect. (At least Burton would have the decency to recite *Under Milk Wood* for twenty minutes before he passed out, bung in hand.)

Turf: What is put in after you give up on the lawn.

Weed: What you smoke after getting the bill for the Turf.

Family: The people who *ruin* your garden by failing to observe the sanctity of hose timers.

Hardy: Fat fellow who stood next to Laurel. Laurels are surprisingly difficult to grow and despite what the saying might suggest, extremely uncomfortable to rest upon. We suggest you try a pillow or a hardy Banana Chair if outside.

Native: The people we stole the country from. They left the Eucalyptus Tree to its own devices, which is a smarter move than you made when you hired that Tree Lopper to come in. $700 for 10 minutes with a chainsaw! If the fellow had not been holding a chainsaw when he gave us the bill, we would have been tempted not to pay it.

Mulch: Mulch was the Miller's son in *Robin Hood*. Damn fine gardener. Unlike the Sheriff of Nottingham who could never even master a Lavender Plant.

Green Thumb: The colour of your thumb three days after you drop a hoe on it.

Horticulture: Opera and Ballet. Haughty Culture is regularly patronised by Snobby Seniors, but even they do not enjoy it. They are caught in a subscription trap, as each season they move up another row of seats to get closer to the performance that they secretly do not enjoy. Much the same thing occurs with Senior Males and retaining their sacred Membership of the Cricket Ground.

Once these terms are mastered and then forgotten, Senior Gardening can begin in earnest. (No, in the ground, not a person *called* Ernest; in any case they only exist in Oscar Wilde plays for their irony value.) Our firm advice to all Seniors is: *Be Wary of Potatoes*. Almost every new Senior Gardener turns into Sir Walter Raleigh the Second when it comes to their sudden Potato Obsession. A huge portion of your garden will be allotted to these potatoes, you will dote on them, wait forever and then when you dig them up we can guarantee you every guest or family member will be *tremendously* unimpressed:

You: There you are! Fresh from the ground today!

Family Member: Right.

You: You can really *taste the difference* from the ones from the Supermarket, can't you?

Family Member: Oh… *(sensing something more required, then speaking as though patronising an escaped mental patient)* Yes, *yes* you can! *(Thinks: Because the ones from the Supermarket don't taste of dirt and are round, instead of looking like a withered bit of Richard III.)*

You: Ungrateful sod.

Family Member: *(startled)* What?

You: That's what I am planting tomorrow as a base! Next October, we will be eating *fresh Turnips!*

Family Member: Thanks for the warning.

(Family Member exits pursued by a Leaf Blower that you borrowed from fool next door.)

The Garden Centre: Senior Gardeners should also be wary of spending too much time here. You should be at the centre of your own garden, not buying yet more seed packets for Sunflowers. Even Vincent Van Gogh would think you are overdoing the Sunflower thing. You have *12 packets* already; unless you annex the neighbour's garden there won't be any room for them, not that they will need it as you have planted them all permanently in the shade. The clue was in the name, genius. Start again.

The Garden Shed: Beloved of Male Seniors, the Garden Shed acts as more of a hideout than an actual place to keep gardening supplies, unless you count Jack Daniels as a supply. Keith Richards would allow it, but your Senior Wife will get suspicious unless you throw at least a few pots and spades about, along with some Warding Off Bags of Fertiliser that shall keep all Senior Spouses with a sense of smell away.

Oh, and if you are buying multiple bags of expensive fertiliser, do not make any jokes about them being for 'terrorist practice'. It may seem like a harmless jest, but many ASIO agents are keen gardeners, spend more time than you would think at Bunnings, and will leap upon the chance to seize high-quality fertiliser on a National Security pretext.

Types of Garden

Despite what your own chaotic hodgepodge might suggest, gardens can be both *themed* and *planned*. The fellow who came up with this idea was called 'Capability Brown', so named because he was capable of getting any aristocrat to give him tons of cash to turn their previously beautifully manicured lawns into a ramshackle English 'Landscape Garden'.

This is in turn led to great opportunities for English 'Landscape Painting'; before then all English paintings were of Upper Class Ladies whose necks were too long and were done by either Joshua Reynolds or Thomas Gainsborough, with ne'er a Hay Wain to be seen.

This all changed instantly, or in about three years if you hired Capability Brown, who took his sweet time, thus setting the precedent for all future Landscape Gardeners. Anyway, the following types of garden might look nice surrounding your Senior Chateau:

Ornamental Gardens: These gardens can be quite lovely depending on what type of ornaments you have. The simplest patch of daisies can be dazzling if you toss a few Fabergé Eggs in there. Tiffany Lamps can also bring colour to any dull water feature, although be careful turning them on if you are not earthed properly. Yes, we realise you are standing on the Earth but that is part of the problem; if you could flick the lamp on in mid-air you would be home free, but even Russian Gymnasts find this difficult to pull off over a water feature without a really long run-up.

Flower Gardens: The coward's way out. We can all pop off to the Nursery and plop Lilacs, Shrubs and Tea Roses everywhere, but is this *really* gardening? This is buying and maintenance and Capability Brown would be ashamed of you. Now, if you do it from *scratch*, that is something else and can be very absorbing.

We have known Seniors who have spent more time on raising Roses than they did raising their Children. This is not as foolish as it sounds, the Roses are often much better company, cost less and have a better chance of getting into a decent Law School. One bunch of Two-Tone Reds we know got pre-approved for Bond University last November. (Yes, it is only Bond University, but still pretty good considering.)

Japanese Gardens: These are quite lovely, but you will have to emigrate, learn a new language and avoiding bringing up the subject of Harry Truman.

Woodland Gardens: The essence of these gardens is apparently 'a sense of informality'. In our experience, *most* gardening is informal,

formal dress rarely being seen anywhere near a wheelbarrow. We know of very few Seniors who still wear even a tie in their yard, much less Top Hat, White Tie and Tails, but if you are one of these Fred Astaire types, then think twice before committing fully.

Rock Gardens: Even lazier than the Flower Garden people. Rocks require extremely little maintenance and unless you are extremely stupid, no watering whatsoever. Rocks do grow, but as we recall from school, they do this *very* slowly, indeed by the use of Tectonic Plates, which are definitely not Dishwasher Safe. Of course, if your home is located next to an active Volcano, your Rock Garden may grow faster. The residents of Pompeii all had instant Rock Gardens, but none of them were particularly pleased at the time or subsequently. Avoid.

Water Gardens: Any uneven garden can become a Water Garden with liberal use of a hose. Water Gardens were very popular with Monet, but he rarely painted the mosquitos or his lovely Mademoiselles slapping themselves and bad temperedly yelling 'No, I said I wanted *Tropical Strength* Aeroguard, Claude!' every five minutes. This will be your life if you have a Water Garden.

Herb Gardens: Fun but they got Paul McCartney into a lot of trouble in the 1970's. Then again he did some of his best work during this time. *Band on the Run* has quite a lot of Herb Garden influence and the whole album still sounds like a cracker. Do not overindulge, or you may write *'Ebony and Ivory'* or *'(Simply Having a) Wonderful Christmastime'*.

Senor Foliage to Be Avoided at All Costs

Ivy: Very nice for Sandstone Universities, if left unwatched for more than eight minutes ivy will wrap itself around every shared fence in the neighbourhood and you will spend the remainder of your days '*just trimming it back a bit*'. This is like trying to give a Hippie a haircut at the height of Woodstock; it will grow faster than you can cut and eventually you will be trapped helplessly by it and will have to listen to the entire set of Country Joe and the Fish before you can hack yourself free.

Bamboo: Makes Ivy look as slow and stoned as Paul McCartney in the '70s. My God does this stuff grow fast. You start off with a nice Zen feel in just a smidge of the garden, and within three weeks you are desperately illegally importing Pandas in the hope they can eat a path to your front door. Stick to grass, like Paul McCartney did until they busted him in Japan.

CHAPTER 22

Date Yourself: The Senior Moments Quiz

YOU BOUGHT, STOLE OR WERE GIVEN THIS BOOK SO OBVIOUSLY you are a Senior, but *how* Senior are you? This quick quiz will give you your Official Senior Score. 10 points for each correct answer.

1. What was the title of the last album you purchased?
   a.   *ABBA's Greatest Hits*
   b.   *A Hard Day's Night*
   c.   *Songs for Swingin' Lovers!*
   d.   Can't remember the name, but it was the last 78 before Al Jolson popped his clogs

2. What time do you eat dinner?
   a.   6 pm
   b.   5.30 pm
   c.   1 pm. 6 pm for tea
   d.   When I'm good, Nurse promised

3. Which famous comic book character are you old enough to remember first appearing in the newspaper?
   a.   Charlie Brown
   b.   Ginger Meggs

    c.   Fatty Finn

    d.   Pig Iron Bob

4. Which of these people were married to Elizabeth Taylor?

    a.   Richard Burton

    b.   Richard Burton

    c.   Robert Taylor

    d.   Lassie

5. Who can you remember becoming a Celebrity Couple?

    a.   Brad and Jen

    b.   Eddie and Debbie

    c.   Bogie and Bacall

    d.   Adam and Eve

6. When did you learn to drive?

    a.   When there were no seatbelts

    b.   When there was no air conditioning

    c.   When there were no turn signals

    d.   When Mr Ford said the Model T was nearly ready

7. How do you refer to big screen entertainment?

    a.   The Pictures

    b.   The Flicks

    c.   The Talkies

    d.   Magic Lantern Shows

8. When people say 'The War', what war do you first think of?

    a.   Vietnam

    b.   Korea

    c.   WWII

    d.   The Battle of Balaclava

9. Drinking was more fun before:

a. Low carbohydrate beer was invented

b. Breath Testing began

c. The six o'clock swill ended

d. Eliot Ness shut down Al Capone

10. You can remember when the definition of a 'bad girl' was:

a. A lady who wore no stockings

b. A lady who smoked

c. A lady who ignored the names written on her dance card

d. Mata Hari

11. When you were a child, you worried about getting:

a. Mumps

b. Polio

c. Rickets

d. The Black Death

Check your answers at the bottom of the page.

Answers: You've forgotten your answers, haven't you? Start again.

CHAPTER 23

Senior Moments with the Royal Family

ALL SENIORS, WHETHER RABID REPUBLICANS OR CONSERVATIVE Constitutional Monarchists, have grown up with the Royal Family. They are the regal soap opera that has played out for our entire lives, long before *The Crown* ever thought of writing some of it down and putting it on Netflix. Let us therefore examine the highlights and lowlights of Senior Life with The Windsors.

1936: Edward VIII Abdicates the Throne: This threw everybody, particularly George VI, who was expecting to live a quiet life stuttering in the countryside. Edward resigned his office because he was in love with Mrs Simpson (Wallis not Marge) and as King, he was not allowed to marry a divorcée. This seemed odd, particularly as Henry VIII had started the entire Protestant Religion to get divorced whenever he liked. Before this, Henry had to behead all of his wives, which was messy, time consuming and, in the case of Jane Seymour, ruined the possibility of retakes in *Live and Let Die*.

As it turned out, it was probably a good thing he did resign, as Edward VIII seemed rather too fond of the Führer, which would have made WW2 either very short or very awkward. Edward VIII spent the rest of his life dressing immaculately, visiting casinos and briefly being Governor of the Bahamas, which was not a terribly taxing job as they had no tax system whatsoever.

As for Wallis Simpson, she would occasionally turn up at Royal Funerals so that the Queen Mother could glare at her, but apart from that did very little apart from penning a memoir entitled *The Heart Has Its Reasons*. Spoiler alert: her reason was she wanted to do it with the Prince of Wales.

1941: Buckingham Palace is Bombed: A big deal at the time, though not for Winston Churchill who got bombed every night. 'Finally,' said the Queen, 'we shall be able to look the East End in the face.' It does make one wonder where she was looking at them before. Also, how often did the Royal Family pop past the East End? The theatres were all in the West End and all the good restaurants were in Piccadilly. Actually, all the good restaurants were in Paris, but that was being occupied at the time. As for Princess Elizabeth, she was in the Woman's Auxiliary Corps learning how to drive a jeep, making her the first female Royal to be part of the Armed Forces, although Queen Victoria was briefly used as a Tank during the Battle of Spion Kop.

1947: The Royal Wedding (the one that lasted): Princess Elizabeth became betrothed to Prince Philip of Greece, an exceptionally good-looking young man who was once found in a good mood for twenty minutes in June of '45 and never made that mistake again. Prince Philip renounced his citizenship, all of his titles and several of his totties to mark the gravity of the occasion. Phil and Brenda may have had their ups and downs, but they are still married, which is more than you can say of their children except Prince Edward, we think.

What happened to Prince Edward? One seldom hears anything about him. There was a dreadful period in the mid-'80s where he was employed by Andrew Lloyd Webber in an outfit called the 'Really Useful Group', a cruel piece of sarcasm that was beneath Lord Webber, and he thoroughly deserved that recent remake of *Cats*. Did you see it? No, nobody did. We gave up after *Starlight Express* ourselves.

1951: Elizabeth Becomes Queen: As Seniors will remember, Queen Elizabeth learnt that she was now the Queen while staying in a Treehouse in Kenya, which gives you an idea of how much time Phil the Greek spent booking travel accommodation in advance.

The Coronation of a new female Monarch was not without controversy as it was suggested by Louis Mountbatten that the Royal House be called the 'House of Mountbatten', but Prince Philip wanted the Royal House to be called the 'House of Edinburgh'. It took the wisdom of Prime Minister Winston Churchill to point out that the Royal House was called Buckingham Palace and that the Queen's last name was Windsor.

The coronation was televised for the first time and the last time actually; Liz still is the Queen and seems in tip-top shape, knock on wood. Honestly, what an amazing life: her first P.M. was Winnie and her latest one is Boris. If she ever wrote a remotely candid autobiography it would outsell *Harry Potter* in about three seconds.

The Entire 1950's: Princess Margaret is Forbidden to Get Married: She wanted to marry Group Captain Peter Townsend, which was completely unacceptable because the Group he was Captain of was The Who. Although Pete Townsend was a hell of a guitar player, he was also divorced, and according to the C of E was not allowed to marry anyone, even Wallis Simpson. A distraught Princess Margaret was offered Keith Moon instead, who was extremely single, but she said no after he drove his Rolls-Royce into a swimming pool, narrowly missing two corgis.

Princess Margaret offered to resign the throne, until it was pointed out that she didn't have one. It was a tragic affair, although we would note that Princess Margaret made up for it by having heaps of affairs later, including one with Peter Sellers, which must have been fun, especially if he did all his voices. She did get married in 1960 to Lord Snowden, but neither of them took it terribly seriously; he focused on photography mainly, although often his pictures were not strictly in focus which was all right because by this time it was the '60s.

1954: The Queen Visits Australia: Rapturous crowds everywhere. Prime Minister Sir Robert Menzies was particularly impressed, remarking, '*I did but see her passing by, and yet I love her 'til I die*'. This was unwelcome news to both the Queen and Dame Pattie, who thought it was understood this was merely a social visit. We don't blame Sir Robert, Her Majesty was a bit of a peach back in the day, but Prince Philip was standing *right there*, should have picked his moment better.

1972: Princess Anne is Nearly Kidnapped: After a charity do, Princess Anne and her then husband, Mark Phillips, were heading back to Buck Palace in a limo when the car in front, a Ford Escort, stopped short and a man named Ian Ball emerged with a gun, shot Princess Anne's bodyguard (don't worry, he survived) and ordered the Princess to exit the car. '*Not bloody likely!*' was her Royal answer (she had obviously listened closely to her father throughout childhood) and Princess Anne scarpered out the other way to the footpath with her hubby in tow.

Having the luck of the Gods, a former boxing champion named Ron Russell happened to be walking past at this exact moment and he punched Mr Ball in the head and knocked him out. Medals all round, except for Ball, obviously.

Following this, Princess Anne competed for Great Britain as an Equestrian in the 1976 Olympics. Famously, she was the only athlete not to be given a Sex Test, as the officials figured she had grown up in the same palace as Princess Margaret and so would know all about sex. We have always liked Princess Anne and semi-hope another kidnap attempt occurs, just to see what she would do this time.

1981: Chuck and Di Get Married: Prince Charles, who had spent most of his adult life listening to the *Goon Show* and playing Polo – often both at the same time to the distress of his teammates – finally found the girl he wanted to marry. Her name was Camilla Parker Bowles and unfortunately she was already taken, so he married a gorgeous 20-year-old kindergarten teacher named Diana Spencer.

It was the Wedding of the Century, watched by over 750 million people, which meant that Westminster Abbey was bloody crowded. Everybody remembers the Royal Wedding, it was a lovely day, they seemed very much in love and Elton John did *not* sing throughout the entire ceremony, which was the icing on the cake.

As we know, the marriage went a bit pear-shaped to say the least, but all envied the gorgeous shape of Princess Diana as she stepped from her carriage and Earl Spencer tottered her down the aisle. Her train was 26 feet long and had to stop at Paddington Station on the way to the Archbishop.

Famously, Princess Di said Prince Charles's names *in the wrong order* during the wedding vows, but she fared better than he who said 'I take thee, Camilla' twice before Randy Andy had to give him a tap on the shoulder and whisper the correct answer.

1983: An Intruder Gets into the Queen's Bedroom: This startled the Queen who thought for one ghastly moment that it might be Prince Philip under the mistaken impression he was back in the good books. It turned out to be a lunatic named Michael Fagan who had scaled the 14-foot-high wall of Buckingham Palace, and climbed up a drainpipe and into the Queen's bedchamber.

The Queen talked calmly to Fagan about his adventures with the Artful Dodger and Oliver for about 15 minutes before summoning a chambermaid. The Chambermaid said 'Fancy' and turned a little red. 'Excuse me, Your Majesty, for taking of the *liberty*, but *marmalade* is tasty if it's *very thickly spread.*' The Queen replied that this was not an A.A. Milne poem, it was serious and the police were summoned to remove the intruder.

They also removed a man named Anthony Armstrong-Jones, who claimed he was actually Lord Snowden, but the only photographic identification he could produce was so out of focus he was forced to leave until further developments.

1986: Fergie and Andrew Get Hitched: Sarah Ferguson, a boisterous redhead who seemed like a lot of fun, got married to Prince Andrew and instantly became 'tabloid fodder'. This started off innocently enough, ski-fighting with Princess Di in Austria while Prince Charles stared on using the Patented Windsor Glare, but things degenerated fast and soon Fergie was writing endless children's books about 'Budgie The Flying Helicopter' and having her toes sucked by some balding American financier on a tropical island.

No, we are not making this up, Young People, the toe-sucking incident took up the front page of every magazine in the world for at least a month and created a blizzard of punning headlines e.g. *'A Toe Tale Disaster'*, *'Toe Tally Inappropriate'*, *'This Little Piggy Went To Suck It'* and many weighty follow-up articles e.g. *'Are Catholics Allowed to Suck Their Toes? — Malcom Muggeridge Weighs In'*.

1992: Squidgygate: Royal Scandal reached a new low when Prince Charles and Princess Diana both insisted on having all their mobile phone calls with their respective lovers taped and taken immediately to *The Sun* or *The Mirror*.

It was fascinating and quite saucy. Some of the things that Prince Charles said to Camilla we still can't believe and cannot even hint at in a semi-respectable publication such as this one. (All right, here's a clue: Prince Charles wished that he could be an instrument of personal hygiene for Camilla. No, not soap, but you are getting warm, as the Princess said to the Squidgy.)

Funnily enough, at one stage Princess Diana did not think that Prince Charles was having an affair with Camilla, suspecting instead their children's nanny, Tigger Leggy-Bourke, who was very leggy and good friends with Winnie the Pooh. These suspicions were unfounded, unlike the suspicions about Princess Diana whose affairs became so numerous that everyone, including her, lost track.

We are pretty sure she dated a handsome Pakistani surgeon and possibly the Captain of the English Rugby Team, but to be honest it could have been the Captain of the Pakistani Rugby Team and a mildly attractive English chiropodist; they were arriving thick and fast at one point. It was clear to all that it was not a very happy marriage, even by Windsor standards. Princess Diana famously said in her *Panorama* Special that 'there were three people in this marriage'; we believe she was undercounting by at least a dozen.

It was decided to divorce but the tragic rewriting of '*Candle in the Wind*' was only a few months away. It stayed in the charts *forever* too; we longed for '*How Much Is That Doggie in the Window?*' to make a comeback. Even '*Agadoo*' would have been welcomed back with open arms.

(Look, is it just us, or every time you look at red-headed Prince Harry don't you *immediately* think about that red-headed Polo Player chap who was very close friends with Diana in the mid-'80s? I mean seriously, how many red-headed Royals can you think of? Even Bonnie Prince Charlie had jet black hair. *Hmm*.)

CHAPTER 24

Senior Moments in Retirement Transition

It is often said that the mortality rate for Senior Men is highest during their first year of retirement. This is because their wives strangle them.

The transition from being a high-powered dynamo at the office to figuring out how to use Dynamo on their navy trousers is a difficult one, especially as many Senior Men have never voluntarily set foot in the Laundry during their natural lives and still half-think it might be called the Pantry. (Well, pants *are* often in there, it's not entirely stupid. We once knew a Senior Man who made it to the age of 68 before realising that 'Closet' was the correct name for what he had been calling the 'Close-It'.)

Working Senior Women find the step to retirement much easier, as they are finally free of all the high-powered male buffoons who used to think they ran your office.

Many Seniors hope to cling on indefinitely at work, claiming that it gives them a sense of '*purpose*'. The purpose is hiding from their spouses, but eventually the Non-Seniors of your workplace will figure this out, along with your Actual Age and you will be presented with a thickly iced retirement cake with the thoughtful words 'Good Luck!' written on it as you are written off and gradually eased out the door.

Senior Mistakes to Avoid in the Transitional Retirement Phase

1. Building a Bird Bath. Recently Retired Seniors are obsessed with this notion. Why? Have Birds ever built a bath for you? No, they literally poo on you from a great height. Do not become a Bird Enabler by constructing some elaborate Bird Bidet so they feel refreshed and emboldened to continue their filthy habits.

2. Bird Watching. See above. Why are you so obsessed with Birds all of a sudden? Having spent their actual Lifetime at work, Recently Retired Bird Watchers become crazed with the 'Lifetime Tally' of how many different birds they can clock up before they cark it. (Let us hope they are not tallying a Vulture when this sad day comes.)

We hate to break it to you, Recently Retired Bird Watcher, but a) no one is interested, and b) most of you are cheating. Yes, you are; that 'Rusty Coloured Eastern Towhee' *was* a Robin and you *know it*. If you want a pointless Senior Hobby that consists almost entirely of cheating, try Solitaire. It can be done inside and you don't have pretend that your 'camera jammed' when Suspicious Seniors ask for proof of your daily triumphs.

3. Becoming an All-Knowing Sage. This is the result of reading the newspaper far too closely. Previously, the Working Senior would glance at the headlines, read the gossip column/horoscopes and, if male, turn to the sports. Now, the Recently Retired Senior knows all and consequently sees all.

Everything from solving World Hunger, choosing the correct spin-off vehicle for Scarlett Johannsson's *Black Widow* character, or even a trifle like settling the Israeli–Palestinian Conflict once and for all can be explained by asking the Recently Retired

Senior, who can talk seemingly endlessly about any and all of these subjects as you carefully back away.

It does wear off, but Senior Spouses are advised to watch carefully lest the problem evolve into Listening to Talkback Radio, for which there is no cure, apart from deafness.

4. Writing Letters to The Editor. Unlike Millennials, who prefer to keep their abuse short and anonymous through the gift of Twitter, Recently Retired Seniors prefer to complain in paragraph form, with their actual name attached.

This is often a by-product of being an All-Knowing Sage but even Seniors who never read the paper get the urge to bang out a few sentences on the inability of Council to fix the jammed post office box two streets over even though it has been *three years*, ending with some stinging mock verse (*'Through rain, hail, snow and sleet, this council shall do nothing, as it is asleep.'* **Simone Elliot, Pymble**). Writing Letters to the Editor is a lot of fun and gives the Editor something to do, as they are clearly not reading or changing the guff that clogs up your local rag, but the Retired Senior should limit themselves to one letter a month, otherwise they will become a Current Crank.

5. Compiling a Family Tree. Oh God. As Joyce Kilmer wrote so beautifully, 'I think that I shall never see, something a boring as a Family Tree'. Family Trees result in the destruction of many real trees for no good purpose as they are never read by any member of the Family except the one who compiled it. The Recently Retired Senior may well discover that their Great-Great-Great Aunt's Niece briefly married the Brother of Louisa May Alcott's Second Cousin Once Removed, but this may not be greatly or even briefly interesting to any other human on the planet.

Even if you dug up the author of *Little Women* and somehow managed to revive her, we doubt she would give a stuff. Oh, and if you do go ahead and try compiling a Family Tree do not be surprised if you get a very cool reception from any surviving Even More Senior Relatives. As you know, despite what young people think, sex was not invented yesterday and you will be amazed at the number of faded wedding and birth dates that are not exactly separated by nine months or anywhere near it.

Much like Sleeping Dogs, it is best to let the Past lie, or at least fudge a birthdate without you drawing attention to the fact the Great Aunt Mabel was a horndog and had a shotgun marriage.

6. Going Back 'Part-Time'. Many Seniors cannot accept that they are now married to retirement, and will try to begin an affair with work called 'Part-Time'. However, unlike a real affair, there is an excellent chance that your Senior Spouse will approve. Be careful, or you may become a Semi-Retired Senior, who is caught between two stools. (Literally, they installed ergonomic stools instead of chairs the day after you left. And changed all the computers to Apple instead of Microsoft Word. *Dammit, what is right click on this thing?*)

7. Going 'Full Kondo'. What Seniors used to call 'throwing stuff out' has now been turned into a near religion called 'The KonMari Method' by the charming, attractive and slightly giggly Organisation Sensation, Marie Kondo. The central Kondo technique is to examine each item in your house and ask *'Does it spark Joy?'* If not, get rid of it. (No, a spouse does not count as an item.)

It may sound like a harmless method of tidying up and an airtight excuse for getting rid of that speckled vase your Mother-in-Law bought as an engagement present, but if performed by the Grumpy Senior in a particularly Joyless mood, it can result in your house being as empty and echoey as a Regional Art Gallery.

Also, there is a real risk that while going through each item in the house the Senior Male may stumble across the love letters you kept from your University Beau that you claim you never even think about anymore. God, he was dishy. And, although he had terrible handwriting, the Senior Male will be able to read enough to have argument ammunition for at least a decade, especially if he finds the one about what your Beau would like to do with test tubes in the Chem Lab when you are finally alone.

That did indeed spark Joy, and an alarming phosphorescence that alerted a Senior Lecturer down the corridor and led to your Beau's expulsion. (Technically, his second of the evening.) Beware.

8. Joining Neighbourhood Watch. Yes, it sounds civic-minded and you secretly hope it will be a bit exciting like *Rear Window* but really it results in other members of Neighbourhood Watch tapping on *your* Rear Window and informing you that your Front Porch Light is broken. God almighty, so over dramatic, couldn't they have just knocked on your front door to tell you this? *What kind of a pathetic, bored busybody...* oh.

9. Watching American Soap Operas. It will start as an ironic lark. 'How ridiculous!' you will chortle as various hunks and lovelies chew up the scenery and each other. But you will watch once more, *just for fun*. And another. And now you are fully invested as to whether Brooke will wake up from her coma, again, and whether Prince Omar should fulfil his moral obligation to Ridge and tell him that he knows Ridge's shipwrecked bride, the amnesiac woman they both love, is still alive.

These Soap Opera guys know what they are doing: the shows are more addictive than heroin and unlike heroin are delivered free to your house every day at 2.30 pm. Do not call then, I am busy. *Omar, damn Royal Protocol, you can marry a divorcée, summon your courage and dismiss your advisers at once, you fool!*

10. Reading *War and Peace*. The reverse of the Soap Opera problem, but equally devastating to the self-esteem of the Recently Retired Senior. All your life you have sworn that one day, when you have time, you will read Tolstoy's *War and Peace*. You are a cultured person, you watched *Brideshead Revisited*, including the boring episodes after Sebastian and his teddy bear left.

All right, here we go, *Chapter One*. Oh, it's the title page first, *War and Peace by Leo Tolstoy*. Upon reading the title page you realise that *War and Peace* is not just one book, it is in fact 15 books (in Roman numerals) and not one, but two, separate epilogues. You are undaunted, you once read *Middlemarch*, or at least faked your way through an essay about it at High School in the middle of March. No more delay, let us begin:

BOOK ONE: 1805: CHAPTER I

'Well, Prince, so Genoa and Lucca are now just family estates of the Buonapartes. But I warn you, if you don't tell me that this means war, if you still try to defend the infamies and horrors perpetrated by that Antichrist – I really believe he is Antichrist – I will have nothing more to do with you and you are no longer my friend, no longer my "faithful slave", as you call yourself! But how do you do? I see I have frightened you...'

How on earth did Tolstoy know that we were frightened? He *is* good. We haven't even finished the first paragraph yet and a cold sweat has begun to break out. You are brave, and like Tolstoy for the next 1,800 pages, you shall continue:

'"... sit down and tell me all the news." It was in July, 1805, and the speaker was the well-known Anna Pávlovna Schérer, maid of honor and favorite of the Empress Márya Fëdorovna. With these words she greeted Prince Vasíli Kurágin...'

All right that's it. We are 12 lines in and have encountered at least three names, one umlaut and four accents we haven't a hope in hell of remembering, let alone pronouncing, even internally. Like Napoleon in Moscow 756 pages from now, we know when we are beaten.

On no account should the Surrendered Senior try to recover some pride by reading *Moby Dick*. It starts off much better with a very short sentence: 'Call me Ishmael' and ends very well *(spoiler alert)* with a scene involving a whale being speared, but in between there is a hell of a lot of stuff about *cetology*, which is the zoological classification of whales.

We can't prove this, but we are pretty sure that Herman Melville just wanted to write an encyclopaedia called *Everything I Know About Whales* and then gave in to some Publisher's request to turn it into a novel by poking a spear of story in at hundred-page intervals. The fact that the name of one of the main characters is *Queequeg* and that the boat is called *Pequod* suggests that Melville did not spend a lot of time re-drafting the non-whale bits.

We strongly suggest that the Recently Retired Senior give up with this high-falutin' stuff and get stuck into some *'Jack Reacher'* books by Lee Child. Jack Reacher is a super cool ex-US Army Major who is also Recently Retired. He travels the country hitchhiking and never goes more than 15 pages without fighting six guys at the same time or making love with a beautiful and powerful woman. Sometimes he does both at once, Reacher is that good. Seriously, they are great fun, get on it.

CHAPTER 25

Senior Moments in Rock 'n' Roll

AMONG THE MANY THINGS SENIORS HAVE WITNESSED COME and go is 'Rock Music'. Seniors were there when Elvis first wiggled onto the scene and we were also there when it ended, which must have been a while ago as we have not heard an actual electric guitar in a song for at least a decade. Please refresh your Senior Memories with the following highlights.

Bill Haley and His Comets: Apart from discovering the Comet, which made a somewhat disappointing appearance in 1986 as Seniors who stayed up late with a telescope for no reason will recall, Mr Haley also accidentally discovered *Rock 'n' Roll*. Previously leading a happily obscure existence in a boogie-woogie combo, Bill recorded a peppy song in 1954 called '*Rock Around the Clock*'. They put it over the opening credits of *Blackboard Jungle* with Glenn Ford and riots instantly broke out amongst teenagers all over the globe.

This was a shock to Bill, who despite having a 'Kiss-Curl' also had middle-aged spread and was clearly far too old for this sort of thing. He and the Comets gamely tried to keep the ruse up with boogies like '*Razzle Dazzle*' and '*See You Later, Alligator*' but it was clear that Bill was as mystified as the rest of the adult world as to what the hell just happened. What happened was:

Elvis Presley: The King of Rock 'n' Roll, the truck driver from Memphis who shocked everyone by moving his *entire body* in a *very* suggestive manner on stage. Previously, the sexiest any white singer had got was when Frank Sinatra leant forward five inches at Radio City Music Hall and raised his left pinky.

Elvis did a lot more than that, teenage girls and their fathers both started screaming at once and he was soon too sexy to be filmed from the waist down on *The Ed Sullivan Show*. The waist up was sexy enough as it was. He was handsome as hell, wore gold suits, had long greasy hair, short greasy songs and was fantastic in every conceivable way, including giving you tips on how to conceive whenever he sang *'Hound Dog'* and moved his hips.

For some reason, going from being a 19-year-old dirt-poor Assistant Delivery Boy to the Most Famous and Richest Singer in the History of the Universe threw Elvis a little. Fortunately, Colonel Tom Parker was there to take half of Elvis's money and place him in the Army for a few years so we could all calm down.

Once Elvis got out of the Army, the Colonel calmed things down further with a two-part plan:

1) Stopping Elvis from giving concerts entirely (an unconventional management strategy for the hottest singer in the world, but we were *sure* the Colonel knew what he was doing)

2) Putting Elvis in an endless succession of gradually more terrible movies. (We began to *permanently* lose faith in the Colonel's managerial skills at this point.)

This is not entirely fair. Elvis was great in *Viva Las Vegas* with the equally great Ann-Margret, and *Girl Happy* is also a fun romp if you ever get the time, but there was no getting around the fact that the guy who belted out *'Jailhouse Rock'* and *'Blue Suede Shoes'* like a miracle was now half-heartedly singing such immortal classics as *'Do the Clam'* and *'There's No Room To*

Rhumba in A Sports Car'. (The latter was patently untrue, those cars were enormous in the '60s, a mixed party of eight could do the Tango in the backseat of a Pink Cadillac for a start.)

Things perked up in 1968 when Elvis defied the Colonel and did the *Elvis Comeback Special*, but soon after Elvis discovered the McDonald's Cheeseburger Special and it was all downhill in ever-expanding jumpsuits from there.

Little Richard: An outrageous performer in every possible way, Little Richard's songs were so filthy you could not even work out how dirty they were. Do you know what '*A Wop Bop A Loo Bop, A Wop Bam Boom*' even means? Neither did we, but we loved it. Little Richard knew a girl name Sue, who '*knew just what to do*'. We knew lots of girls named Sue, they had no idea of what to do and, even if given an instructional pamphlet, had no intention of doing it with us anyway.

It did seem a shame that Little Richard could not lend us one of his many ladies, as he himself seemed more interested in his hair than in the fairer sex. In fact, Richard considered himself the fairer sex and he had an excellent case: no subsequent Rock Star used eyeliner half as well; he made Mick Jagger look like a bag lady.

Little Richard had smash after smash, wrote his own stuff and his voice was amazing but we still can't believe he got away with lyrics in 1955 like '*Good golly Miss Molly, sure like to ball*'. That was the *opening line* of the song! What did the Older Generation think he meant? Did they really believe that Miss Molly was fond of ballroom dancing? In which case, why was she so busy '*rocking and a rolling, can't hear her Momma call*'?

Richard's not terribly carefully hidden agenda was also displayed in songs like '*Long Tall Sally*', a scorcher about a transvestite prostitute, and '*Tutti Frutti*', a wonderfully joyful song about how great it was to have gay sex.

Ahead of his time by about a million years, today's Seniors all loved him, yesterday's Seniors lived in blissful ignorance and he seemed unstoppable. Unfortunately, and this is true, when he was touring Australia in 1957, Little Richard saw Sputnik cross the skies for the first time, had an instant Religious Conversion, threw $100,000 worth of jewellery into the nearest river, gave up Rockstardom and became a Pentecostal Preacher! Well, the man knew how to make an exit.

(We know what you are wondering: the river he threw the jewellery into was the Hunter, in Newcastle, and *no*, there is probably no point looking now.)

Buddy Holly: One of the most talented writers in Rock history, penning '*Rave On*', '*Every Day*', '*Peggy Sue*', '*Words of Love*', '*Not Fade Away*' and '*Maybe Baby*' before the age of 23. As all Seniors know, Buddy did not actually make it to 23, tempting fate by writing '*That'll Be The Day (When I Die)*' and taunting the laws of aerodynamics by getting on a small plane with a man called The Big Bopper.

Yes, we know Ritchie Valens was there too, but he was 17 and weighed about 120 pounds with guitar in hand. The real bugger of it is that the Big Bopper only had one hit, and although we love '*Chantilly Lace*', the world could have bopped along perfectly well if he alone had bought the Dirt Farm early.

Even if he did survive, we doubt the Big Bopper would have fared well in the 'Me Too' era, with his explicit penchant for a 'wiggling walk', a 'giggling talk' and a 'ponytail hanging down'. These three things alone made him act like a long-necked goose and further questions would have been asked about why a 30-year-old DJ was so obsessed with schoolgirls in general.

Buddy Holly, on the other hand, was a tragic loss. He was so great at writing songs he had two more hits *after* he died; his manager thoughtfully, if not tastefully, dubbing The Crickets onto dead Buddy's demos of 'Crying, Waiting, Hoping' and 'Peggy Sue Got Married', literally both just recorded by Buddy in a hotel cupboard. Holly also inspired hits after he was dead, most famously in 'American Pie' by Don McLean, who was probably aware that this was the dessert that had made the Bopper so Big in the first place.

Don McLean also wrote 'Vincent (Starry, Starry Night)', but we do not blame the Big Bopper for that fatality, although he did nothing to *help* Vincent either and openly preferred Gauguin.

Jerry Lee Lewis: 'The Killer', so named because he killed his career stone dead in 1959 by marrying his 13-year-old cousin. Yes, it was legal in the South, but so were many other things, not including having Great Balls of Fire, which would result in prosecution and severe singeing even if you were married to a non-cousin. Jerry Lee Lewis further damaged his career by splitting up with Dean Lee Martin, and although funny in *The Nutty Lee Professor* it was never quite the same.

Chuck Berry: The Poet of Rock. To many, the Father of Rock 'n' Roll and certainly the Father of Recycling. Came up with a wonderful guitar riff for 'Johnny B. Goode' and then re-used exactly the same riff shamelessly in at least 27 other hits.

It wasn't until Chuck began to sing the lyrics that you could even begin to work out which song you were hearing and often you had to wait until the second verse to be entirely sure. Most of his protagonists were called 'Johnny' or 'Maybellene', which didn't help. Got a 65-year career out of it and was duck-walking well into his 90s. You can barely summon up the energy to go duck feeding on a nice day. Shape up.

Chuck had many troubles with the law, including bank robbery as a youth, tax evasion as an adult and a 'Violation of the Mann Act' in 1959, which was the result of transporting a girl across state lines for immoral purposes. Chuck explained to the judge that he was the innocent party, as he was simply motorvatin' over a hill when he saw Maybellene in a Coupe de Ville, but the judge recognised the riff and the explanation and Chuck got three years.

A difficult man to say the least, post-prison Chuck refused to set foot on stage until he was paid *in full, in cash* and after this was done he would promptly leave with the money unless he got an *extra* $10,000 in cash, *right now*. By all accounts he was a shocker, but he wrote '*Brown Eyed Handsome Man*' and '*You Never Can Tell*' so we can forgive him anything.

The Everly Brothers: Like the Andrews Sisters, Phil and Don did not get along terribly well but there is obviously something musically magical about siblings who dream of strangling each other, because when they sang '*Dream*' or anything else they sounded like angels who had been practising close harmony for at least a millennium. Their songs reflected various innocent themes of the '50s; for instance, Narcolepsy in '*Wake Up Little Susie*', Cross-Breeding in '*Bird Dog*' and Human Trafficking in '*Cathy's Clown*'.

We are not quite sure why the Everly Brothers split so dramatically, but we have a feeling it was because of the time Phil started snickering uncontrollably during the climax to '*Ebony Eyes*'.

For those Seniors who can't remember, '*Ebony Eyes*' was a particularly morbid and mostly spoken song, where Don Everly asked various plaintive questions to unhelpful Airport Personnel about why his dark-eyed girlfriend's flight was so late getting in on one stormy, stormy night. When Phil suggested it was probably because she was banging the Big Bopper, a fight broke out on stage with Don decking Phil with his own guitar and then accidentally knocking out Little Susie with a left hook;

although that girl was usually asleep so it did not make much difference.

Bo Diddley: Realised that a 'shave and a haircut, two bits' could be turned into a whole song and made out like a bandit. A shameless self-promoter, Bo Diddley's biggest hit was called *'Bo Diddley'*, a shrewd career move which led to the follow-up hit *'Bo Diddley's a Gunslinger'*, which we doubt was true. For one thing, Bo wore glasses, which was not a good indication, although perhaps the other gunfighters were just vain and could have done with spectacles, too.

Bo unwisely thought he could beat the taxman by writing hits under his wife's name, including Mickey and Sylvia's wonderful *'Love is Strange'*, but unfortunately Bo got divorced soon afterwards and so ended up with Diddley.

Fats Domino: The man Elvis called the 'real king' of Rock 'n' Roll, Fats did start pretty much two years before everyone else. He found his thrill on Blueberry Hill (personally, we have always preferred Strawberry Fields, but each to their own), wrote and sang *'Ain't That A Shame'*, *'Blue Monday'*, and the credibility-stretching smash *'I'm Walking'*.

Fats Domino was so influential that even his name was plagiarised by **Chubby Checker**, who in turn was infuriated by his own obscure imitator, **Big Backgammon**. None of them recorded for Chess Records, which was just as well as it would have been impossible to work out who was winning.

By the by, we have always been intrigued that Chubby Checker had a huge hit with *'Limbo Rock'*. How limber do you think Chubby was? Lovely voice, but when you are taunting us by asking *'How Low Can We Go?'* just remember, Chubby, that we know you are far more familiar with the liquorice stick than the limbo stick.

CHAPTER 26

Senior Moments in Clubs

APART FROM THE BOWLS CLUB, THERE ARE MANY PLACES where like-minded Seniors can gather. The Social Senior can choose from the following selection:

The Masons: Despite what many think, the Masons do not spend all their time secretly running society and holding ancient rituals of the Knights Templar. They also hold the occasional Trivia Night. I would tell you more but, well, you're not a Mason, are you? I can tell by the way you are failing to hold this book in the Sacred Libris Position of the Secret Brotherhood (i.e. *it should be upside down. No, don't change now, you have already been seen, judged and found wanting*).

Rotary: Nice chaps who invented those phones with the whirly dial thing. They do good works, unlike the people who make mobile phones, which seem deliberately made to slip out of your hand and crack the damn screen when they hit the pavement. It was once strongly rumoured that Rotary were puppets of the Masons; which is ridiculous as the Masons do not even use puppets in their secret rituals, although Sooty and Sweep were both members in the late '50s.

The CWA: Do not be intimidated by the Country Women's Association, unless you are attempting to tell them the correct way to make a scone. You are free to join even if you are not from the Country; any outer suburb will do as long as you own flannel of some description (no, a Burberry scarf does *not* count). You do have to be a woman, though, but if you pop a frock on and sit up the back, nobody will ask any questions. Worth it for the free jam alone.

The CWA meets once every two weeks or anytime there is a New Lemonade Scone Recipe worth talking about, which is more often than you would think. The CWA was originally formed to *'alleviate female rural solitude'*, i.e. the properties were so far apart that there was nobody to gossip to, apart from the cows, which was an udder waste of time.

Lions Club: Lower your expectations now, there are no actual Lions in the Club. Big Cats of all description are forbidden from joining, and applications are rarely received in any case and are probably made up, although that letter from somebody claiming to be Kimba had impressive pawmanship. The Lions Club is known for their famous Christmas Cakes and Puddings, which raise enormous sums of money because they are never actually consumed, thus making the productions costs astonishingly low.

Similar to Rotary, the Lions Club has been rumoured to be a *shadow arm of the Masons* but we find this difficult to believe as the Masons do not use Pudding in any of their ancient rituals, they use Haggis, and make frequent use of actual Lions in the Ceremony of The Templar Fire Hoop Jumping. We have probably said too much and await just punishment from any 32nd Degree Mason who is reading this volume upside down right now.

Red Hat Ladies: We have no idea what these spunky ladies do, but they always look like they are having a *terrific* time and behave as though they have had two large glasses of top-drawer champers. Why not buy a Red Hat and find out? You could do with a new hat anyway, your current one looks like it was either worn by Queen Mary or got water damage while *on* the *Queen Mary*. Treat yourself, you are a Senior, you deserve it.

Amway: No, this is not a club and you will *never* be invited to a luncheon party again if you pretend it is or speak another syllable about the incredible system of wealth creation you have discovered.

PROBUS: In this extremely popular social club for Seniors, membership is limited to 70, which is a shame as most members are well over that. We will not hear a bad word said about PROBUS: they attended the hit theatre show *Senior Moments* in droves and we are forever in their debt. Quite literally, actually, as we took out many full-page ads in PROBUS magazines and have not paid up. We are hoping to work out some sort of contra deal in exchange for some Lions Christmas Puddings of which we have several thousand, many from the current millennium.

The Mickey Mouse Club: As a Senior, it is no longer appropriate for you to belong to this club, even though you still have the hat in more or less perfect condition. If you think you have any hope of running into Annette Funicello at a club function, you are sorely mistaken, as Annette left us in 2013. Frankie Avalon is still alive though, sings *'Beauty School Dropout'* like a champ, and is surprisingly affordable for weddings if you ask nicely and throw in a free round of golf.

CHAPTER 27

Senior Moments at the Movies

As CINEMAGOERS, SENIORS TODAY ARE MOSTLY LURED TO THE flicks by various combinations of Judi Dench, Maggie Smith, Bill Nighy, Joanna Lumley and Helen Mirren; usually they are running a hotel in India or competing in a Nude Synchronised Swim Team to raise money for something. Either that or some film with Queen Victoria or Queen Elizabeth (I or II) in it.

Surely it can only be a matter of time before genres combine and we get to see Judi Dench playing Queen Victoria running '*The Best Royal Exotic Hotel Swim Squad*', with a cheeky cameo by Derek Jacobi as a camp bellboy ('I thought somebody pressed my *dinger*!'). (Actually, that's not bad: don't try to pitch this to any Studio Heads, we are way ahead of you.)

There was a time when *all* movies were suitable for Seniors, and there were also actual Movie Stars under 70 whose names we knew. Let us take a trip down Senior Memory Lane and examine some of the Greats that are now forgotten by Netflix-Obsessed Youngsters.

Clark Gable: *The* movie star, he was known as 'The King' five years before Elvis was even born. The King was so popular that when he appeared in the wonderful romantic comedy

It Happened One Night in 1934, Gable caused a sensation by removing his shirt to reveal... *no singlet beneath*! Overnight the singlet industry collapsed, except on building sites, where the singlets remained but the buildings collapsed. Gable was so good looking that even having ears like Dumbo couldn't hold him back and he landed the plum role of Rhett Butler in the biggest film of all time: *Gone With the Wind*.

Now that Clark was signed up, Ace Producer David O. Selznick began his famous *worldwide search for Scarlett O'Hara*. After ten months he *still* couldn't find her and so hired Vivien Leigh to *pretend* to be Scarlett instead.

Selznick was determined to spare nobody else's expense as he created this masterpiece. On one memorable occasion he decided to film the famous 'Burning of Atlanta' scene by buying a tin of petrol and setting fire to the actual Atlanta with his Bic. This made Take 2 a bit of a no-go, although it did look great on screen.

Gone With the Wind ended sensationally too, with Gable's famous last line to Scarlett: *'Frankly, my dear, you can go stuff yourself'* being slightly changed in post-production, a damn good decision by Selznick.

Clark Gable was also married to the great Carole Lombard, making them possibly the most attractive couple in the history of the planet. Sadly, Carole died when her plane crashed while she was raising War Bonds in 1942. (It may have crashed into Glenn Miller's plane, who was doing something similar, but in 3/4 time.) Due to this accident, Movie Stars gave up raising War Bonds and focused on raising Ward Bond instead, which paid off when he was so great in *Wagon Train*.

Bette Davis: In an age where actresses were largely cast on looks rather than talent (how times have changed, *ahem*), Bette Davis survived on her incredible gifts and her incredible eyes. (She was still alive when the song *'(She's Got) Bette Davis Eyes'* was a big hit in 1983, which must have been extremely confusing and redundant for her to listen to.)

Bette Davis was such a great actress that she makes Meryl Streep look like Kim Novak. (Talent wise, we mean, we would all love to *look* like Kim Novak, but impartial observers will admit Jimmy Stewart was doing the heavy lifting in *Vertigo*. Literally as well, a cruel and eccentric man, Hitchcock made Jimmy carry him to the cafeteria every day for lunch, a difficult job on the way there, one shudders to imagine the trip back, especially if cabbage had been consumed by the Master of Suspense, who was definitely not the Master of His Suspenders.)

Bette's signature role was in *All About Eve* where she chewed the scenery, ate Marilyn Monroe for breakfast and beat the hell out of Joan Crawford who wasn't even in the movie.

Many actresses try to emulate Bette today but unless you smoke two packs a day, drink like a fish and have the talent of the Gods, you are wasting your time. Bette Davis also spoke *juuust like Bet-tey Davis,* in an age when all great stars had memorable vocal patterns. Try doing a Julia Roberts impression and see who recognises it, but if you pause appropriately, rasp and say 'Wh*aaa*t a *dump!*' everybody over 60 and all homosexual men instantly know *you are doing Bette Davis.*

Bette acted well into her 70's, and badly into her 80's, which was largely academic as it was difficult to discern her in any film from 1972 onwards because she was surrounded by such a large cloud of cigarette smoke. The Assistant Directors did occasionally summon up the nerve to ask Bette to put the coffin nail out, but one lightning glare from *the* Bette Davis eyes and they ran terrified for the hills. We do not blame them.

Gary Cooper: Look, it wasn't just the actresses who were cast on looks, many of the men were bloody gorgeous in the Golden

Age, too. Gary Cooper began as a star in Silent Movies, and he carried the policy of not taking well into the Talkie Era. Most of Gary Cooper's parts consisted solely of the words '*Yup*', '*Nope*', '*I reckon*' and the occasional '*Guess you'd better be gone by sundown*'. Luckily these few syllables were enough to carry Gary through most Westerns and Romantic Comedies.

Cooper became known as the '*strong and silent type*', although we have yet to see any proof of his feats of strength and doubt if he could even lift Alfred Hitchcock without throwing his back out. Cooper's signature role was in *High Noon*, a unique western that was filmed in *real time*, so that Grace Kelly could make it to Monaco in time for the Rehearsal Dinner.

The plot of the movie revolved around Gary, as a silent sheriff, asking various cowardly townsfolk to help him face down some Bad Eggs at High Noon. (Why were all gunfights always at High Noon? What was wrong with quarter past 11? Surely somebody owned a pocket watch?) Anyhoo, the quivering town residents all refuse, leaving Cooper waiting alone and inaudible on main street at 11.59 am for the thrilling climax.

Incidentally, John Wayne thought that this plot was extremely offensive and believed the film itself to be Communist Propaganda. Of course, the Duke also thought this about *Some Like It Hot* and *Beach Blanket Bingo*, but in this case he may have had a point as the film ends with Grace Kelly singing a rousing rendition of '*The Red Flag*', which always struck us as a little odd.

Katharine Hepburn: A brilliant actress and one of the world's great eccentrics, Katharine Hepburn Shocked the World in the '30s by wearing long trousers instead of dresses. (Admittedly, it did not take much to *shock the world* back then; a lady could go to lunch without white gloves on and the world would clutch its pearls and ask for the smelling salts.)

Despite winning her first Academy Award for Best Actress in 1933 for *Morning Glory*, Hepburn became known as box-office poison, which was unfair as she was never convicted of poisoning anyone at the box office itself, although Merle Oberon swears she saw Kate sprinkling diuretics in the popcorn machine more than once.

Hepburn bounced back triumphantly in the screwball classic *Bringing Up Baby* with the popular Cary Grant and *The Philadelphia Story* also with the popular Cary Grant. She was no fool, and stood next to Cary Grant as much as possible, who also wore long trousers, although not when he was living with Randolph Scott; but that is a story for another day.

Hepburn also had the world's least secret affair with Spencer Tracy; they made eight films together just to give Tracy's wife a pretext for spending all their time together, including *Adam's Rib*, *Pat and Mike*, *We're Having a Secret Affair*, *Woman of the Year*, *Desk Set* and *Yep, We Are Definitely Still Cheating*.

Tracy and Hepburn were one of the great romances, although, being Irish, Tracy was (can you guess where this is heading, dear reader?) *drunk* and *miserable* almost all of the time. *Quelle surprise.* (Once again, if you have not read other chapters of this book, it's fine, the author is also Irish and bombed right now. I could be happier, too, but that is a private matter concerning Charlotte Rampling and myself that I do not wish to speak of.)

Tracy & Hepburn, by this stage sufficiently close to be awarded an ampersand, continued making movies together up until Tracy's death, the last one being *Guess Who's Coming To Dinner?* Being stewed and in his late seventies, Spencer guessed wrongly: he thought it would be Don Ameche and spent most of the last two reels sulking when Sidney Poitier turned up.

Alarmingly talented, Hepburn won four Oscars for Best Actress, deserved at least three more and even out-acted Peter O'Toole in *The Lion in Winter*, which took some doing. (Luckily, being Irish, O'Toole was often *drunk* and *miserable*, so she did get a running start most days.) A woman of great character, Hepburn refused to admit that she had Parkinson's, arm-wrestling any physician who said otherwise, including a surprised Michael Parkinson who wasn't even a doctor.

Her crowning moment came, perhaps, in 1991 when she was interviewed by Phil Donahue for a one-hour NBC special, only to stop the cameras dead 45 minutes in by asking '*Who the hell are you?*' to the clearly startled Mr Donahue. After he revealed his name, Hepburn replied '*Never heard of you,*' and with a gracious wave allowed his questions to continue. By the way, if you ever get the chance to see her two-hour interview with Dick Cavett from 1971, do *not* miss it. She is amazing. Literally wanders into the empty television studio wearing tennis gear, unannounced and a full day early, as the camera crew race to set up their equipment and Dick struggles to think of a coherent question. Desperate for common ground, Cavett reveals that he had a small part in a summer stock production that Hepburn starred in in the mid-'50s. 'Oh *yes,*' replies a pleased Hepburn, recognition dawning at last, followed by a long pause. 'You were *dreadful,* weren't you?'

Cary Grant: The great Cary Grant was born in England, with the name Archibald Leach. He changed names and countries quickly in order to have any hope of getting a career or a tan. He got both and from 1939 to 1962 Cary Grant was officially the Most Tanned Man on Earth, his streak coming to an end when George Hamilton stole his tanning butter while Cary was doing re-shoots on *Charade.*

An incredibly underrated actor, people always accused Cary Grant of 'just playing Cary Grant', which was infuriating as he was actually a pale working-class guy from Bristol named Archie Leach and was *pretending* to be Cary Grant in the first place.

Grant could play an action hero in a Hitchcock thriller like *North by Northwest*, be a charming romantic lead with Deborah Kerr in *An Affair to Remember* or be a comic marvel in *His Girl Friday*, yet he never won an Academy Award, and was only nominated twice for two now forgotten 'serious' films. According to one of his many wives, the lovely Dyan Cannon, Cary did not take this well and literally jumped up and down on the bed during Oscar broadcasts while yelling obscenities at the various actors who did win. We've all done this in our time, but rarely with Dyan Cannon next to us, so he should have counted his blessings.

Ms Cannon, then Mrs Grant, also reported that Cary was an enthusiastic taker of LSD, something to think about next time you watch him freak out during *Arsenic and Old Lace*.

Cary Grant's wonderful accent was neither English nor American, it was *sui generis*; although Cary was generous enough to loan it out to Tony Curtis to make fun of him in *Some Like It Hot*. 'Nobody talks like that,' complained Jack Lemmon, and he was right with one gloriously handsome exception. A bright and witty man, Grant once received a cable from a reporter in the 1960's that read 'HOW OLD CARY GRANT?' He replied: 'OLD CARY GRANT FINE. HOW YOU?'

Despite a career of triumphs, unfortunately Cary's last film was a stinker called *Walk Don't Run*, a 'comedy' about, we kid you not, the housing shortage that took place during the walking competition in the 1964 Tokyo Olympics. Oh boy. Let us never speak of it again and go watch *To Catch a Thief* right now.

CHAPTER 28

Senior Moments in Inheritance

Toying with Your Children For Fun and Pleasure: or How Not to Be Like King Lear (Who Was An Idiot)

One of the great delights of being a Senior is playing mind games with your offspring when it comes to that topic of eternal interest: The Inheritance. Most Adult Children assume that a Senior's estate will be divided equally between them when you pop your clogs; Seniors will find hours of enjoyment can be had by artfully messing with this expectation. Please pay attention to the following basic methods:

Warren Buffett Method: Wait until your Adult Child is in proximity and then pretend to begin reading the newspaper.

You: My, that Warren Buffett is a clever fellow.

Adult Child: *Thinks: Oh great, another talk about investments of yesteryear.* Says: Mmm.

You: Although he is one of the richest billionaires in the world, it says here Buffett has always told his children that he won't leave them *anything* in his will.

Adult Child: *Thinks: What!* Says: What!

You: Yes, Buffett's theory is that living with the expectation of wealth ruins character, so all his children have to be independent, and they are *happier* for it.

Adult Child: *Thinks: Dance fast!* Says: Well, that *might* be true for a billionaire, but not for an ordinary person.

You: *(offended)* Ordinary person? Funny, I have *never* thought of myself as an ordinary person. *(rise steadily and exit thoughtfully)*

This simple gambit will keep all of your Adult Children incredibly attentive for at least a month, and also doing a lot of trash talking about the Sage of Omaha.

The Good Child Method: This can be sprung at any time but works best towards the end of long walk or right after a long dinner.

You: *(sigh)* Leslie Blackwell died last week.

Adult Child: *Thinks: Who the hell is Leslie Blackwell. Man or woman?* Says: That's no good.

You: Apparently the children are upset about the estate.

Adult Child: *Thinks: Okay, this could be important. Pay attention.* Says: Oh really, why's that?

You: Well, the children *thought* they would all be left equal shares.

Adult Child: *Thinks: That's what we think!* Says: Oh, and... uh... were they?

You: *(meaningfully)* No. *(long pregnant pause)* Your sister Sarah has always been such a *good* girl. *(Rise and leave thoughtfully as Adult Child stares in horror.)*

This will not only result in all your Adult Children not named Sarah sucking up to you like nothing else, but Sarah will be extra nice, too. This method can be repeated anytime with the death of another imaginary friend, substituting the name of a new 'good' child as you see fit.

The Watchtower Method: This is a very easy method to employ as Seventh Day Adventists, very polite Senior Ladies mostly, visit every house in the country at least once every month and leave their free magazine *The Watchtower* at the door as you cower inside pretending that you didn't hear the doorbell. Instead of placing *The Watchtower* in the recycling bin as most people do, simply flip through it idly half a dozen times and then leave it on a lounge chair, folded but open to the middle. Now all you have to do is wait until the Adult Child visits.

Adult Child: *Thinks: Oh my God!* Says: *(faux casual)* Oh, what's this?

You: Oh, just some literature Maxine dropped off.

Adult Child: *Thinks: Literature? Maxine? Oh GOD!* Says: *(casually)* Maxine?

You: Yes, she's one of the ladies from the Seventh Day Adventist Church. She's been popping these at the door for years but, well, to be honest I *was* feeling a bit lonely and I just had her in for tea a few months ago and she had some very interesting things to say.

Adult Child: *Thinks: A few MONTHS! Say something, fool!* Says: You were brought up Catholic, weren't you?

You: Well, there are many paths to salvation. Anyway, the Catholic Church has a lot of money; the Adventists, well, they might need some help *(sad pause)* when my time comes.

Adult Child: *Thinks: Bloody Hell!* Says: *(through jolly laughter)* Oh, that's *many* years away! And I hate to hear about you being lonely, I should bring the kids around more often.

You: That would be lovely.

Yes, it will be. And these Grandchild Visits will only increase in pace if you remember to highlight and *underline* various passages in subsequent issues of *The Watchtower* that you leave casually with care around your house. Use a yellow highlighter for maximum effect and write '*True*' randomly in blue biro next to selected passages. Nothing puts the metaphorical fear of God into your Adult Children like the *real* fear of God getting his mitts on *their* inheritance.

The 'Trust' Method: This is a deliciously ironic method as it revolves around the word 'Trust', the exact quality you will watch evaporate from your Adult Children's eyes the more you say it. The Trust Method works best if you are found fretting somewhere; chew on a pair of glasses if you have any or can borrow some from a reasonably hygienic friend.

Adult Child: Says: What's wrong?

You: There's been a complication with the Trust.

Adult Child: *Thinks: Did he say 'Truss' or 'Trust'?* Says: The Trust?

You: Yes, we never wanted you to worry about money when we were gone, so decades ago your mother and I set up a Trust to avoid any possible future Death Duties. We were *assured* there was no problem in locating the account overseas, but, well...

Adult Child: *Thinks: Well what? Finish a sentence, you old ninny!* Says: Is there anything I can do?

You: No. Look, Mum and I have to go off to the Bahamas for a few weeks to sort some things out. I think it's best, legally, if you don't know anything more than that at this stage. *(Exit with brave nod and the Weight of the World on your shoulders.)*

Now you and your Senior Wife get to enjoy a great vacation in the Bahamas with no grumbling from the kids about 'spending their inheritance'; instead they will be grateful at the thought that you are *saving* their inheritance. This ruse can be kept up for years with trips to Switzerland, Bora Bora or Vanuatu as weather and fancy dictate. You simply 'must get to the bottom' of this Trust mess, and trust us, you will enjoy yourselves as you do.

The Skip Method: Now this one is a lot of fun. Best sprung as you look at your grandchildren frolicking somewhere bucolic.

You: Gosh, they are growing up, aren't they?

Adult Child: *Thinks: Duh!* Says: Yes, they sure are.

You: Are you teaching them to be *responsible* with money?

Adult Child: *Thinks: Well, we are trying to get them to steal less from the spare change tin.* Says: They know the value of a dollar.

You: Good. I want them to be prepared when the time comes.

Adult Child: *Thinks: WHAT!* Says: What?

You: Obviously, they won't get the *bulk* of it, until they are 25. Anyway, *(sad yet somehow happy)* gather ye rosebuds while ye may. *(Charge off to play with tiny tots as your Adult Child tries to work out just how much dough their own children have just cost them.)*

Your Adult Children will now flood you with stories of your grandchildren's gross financial incompetence; the phrase *'danger to themselves'* may come up more than once. Just nod wisely, safe in the knowledge that they don't know you have blown most of the inheritance while enjoying yourself at the track.

Sub-Inheritance Fun: Guilt Games

Short of divvying up the dosh for good, there are a variety of inheritance-related activities the Senior will enjoy:

Stickering: This rather morbid practice is one that many Seniors indulge in. In order to 'avoid arguments' *(ho-ho)* over Beloved Pieces of Furniture and even more Beloved Pieces of Jewellery, you give each of your Adult Children a different coloured sticker and get then to pop it on any object they want dibs on when you snuff it. Then after they have all finished and left the house, simply change all the stickers to different items and wait for the fireworks to begin when they next visit.

The Beloved Object Presentation: This works on any Adult Child as long as they are alone with you.

> **You:** Can you keep a secret?
> **Adult Child:** *Thinks: I knew it! Gary was adopted!* Says: Of course.
> **You:** Look, I wanted to give you something *now* so there will be no squabbling over it after I'm gone.

And now lead the agog Adult Child to the nearest cupboard. Inside the cupboard is a dusty box, inside the dusty box is the ugliest and tackiest piece of porcelain you can find at the nearest op shop, preferably a Clown, a Child Holding Balloons or a Dancing Bear. Bring it forth as though it were the Holy Grail.

> **Adult Child:** *Thinks: Urghhh!* Says: *(reverent)* Oh!
> **You:** It was the only thing your Great-Grandmother could smuggle out of Russia.
> **Adult Child:** *Thinks: I thought she was Irish?* Says: Wow.
> **You:** Anyway, I remember how much you used to play with it as a child.
> **Adult Child:** *Thinks: Well, I did have a lot of nightmares as a child.* Says: *(moved)* I remember.
> **You:** I wanted you to have it now. *Tell no one.*

This exercise can be repeated with each child, extra points if you can give them exact copies of the same dreadful Clown, Child or Bear. It will inspire gratitude in your Adult Child and a Sense of Mystery years later as they try to search for the Russian branch of your red-headed family.

The Lost Will: This is an excellent way of getting your furniture moved and cleaned for free. Simply tell your Adult Children that, Silly Billy that you are, you have Lost the Will. You *made sure* to slip it inside a special book, or at the bottom of a secret draw or secreted somewhere, anywhere, that you would like moved and dusted. Your offspring will spring to work, spring-cleaning like navvies to find the damn thing, especially as you explain that you '*meant to get it updated*'.

They will find nothing except extra reserves of elbow grease as you dither about and try not to look delighted at this free maid service. Can be repeated at later intervals as your memory '*returns*', but don't push it too far. They will get suspicious if you say that the sound of mowing the lawn helps you remember.

Related to the Lost Will is the…

Visit to the Lawyer Trick: You can avoid any unwanted task or much promised attendance by announcing, with a solemnity usually reserved for announcing the death of a beloved Monarch, that you would *like* to but you have to Visit the Lawyer.

Adult Child: Why?
You: A small change must be made. *(pause)* Well, small for some. I really should not say any more than that.

And don't; simply head out the door, change into your Golf Clothes at the club and enjoy a round. Works every single time. If your Adult Children start to get wise and ask for the *name* of the lawyer, simply say they are 'an old family friend. As a matter of fact, they were once *engaged* to your mother. That's partly what the trouble is about. I really should not say any more than that.' This is enigmatic enough to keep everyone wondering about their birthright and birth certificates for years.

CHAPTER 29

Senior Moments in Literature

**How to avoid 'Modern Classics' and enjoy
yourself with Safe Classics For Seniors**

Luckily for Seniors, who do not like new things or change in general, there have been no really good books written since *To Kill a Mockingbird* in 1960. Oh yes, Publishers talk a good game and we have had everyone from Joan Didion to Zadie Smith thrust at us over the years, but let's stop kidding ourselves. Don't tell Jonathan Franzen, but the gig is up.

(Yes, we know some people say *Infinite Jest* by David Foster Wallace was a truly great book, but as no human has ever finished it, nobody is really qualified to say. In a related matter, the police are still not sure if Mr Wallace's death was a suicide or not; he *did* leave a note, but they have only made it up to page 273 and are finding it pretty heavy going.)

The following authors and books may be safely read or reread with enjoyment by all Seniors. But get on with it, you are not getting younger.

Charles Dickens

Dickens was a genius who wrote episodically, which was amazing considering that TV wasn't even invented back then. Starting with *The Pickwick Papers*, he would churn out the chapters at an alarming rate which would then be published in monthly instalments and read by the waiting public. Often the public couldn't wait and would stand over his shoulder in long lines to get a glimpse of what Pip was doing to Mr Micawber this week or vice versa.

This infuriated Dickens's rivals like Thackeray, who accused Dickens of being a *'Populist'*; unlike Thackeray, who preferred to be an *'Unpopulist'* and largely succeeded apart from *Vanity Fair*.

With the exception of a distracting tendency to give his characters names like Mrs Tizzyfuzzwinkle and Mr Croppboppit, Dickens's work holds up wonderfully well and his books are so long that most Seniors will have forgotten *at least* 50% of them before and after reading, which makes them most economical.

Highly Recommended: *Great Expectations*. The best one. Pip, Estella, Herbert Pocket, Magwitch and the marvellously macabre Miss Havisham, still wearing her wedding dress at the age of 70. (What a show-off. Yes, it is impressive she can still fit into it, but a lot of us have other things to do than sit-ups and brooding over being jilted at the altar. Not a lot of jilting goes on at the altar these days, most grooms preferring to jilt via text after having met a stripper who *really understands* them at the Bachelor Party.)

Approach With Caution: *Bleak House*. It is not called *Cheerful House* for a reason. Brilliant but a bit depressing, which is unusual for Dickens who preferred to keep things upbeat. Even when Bill was beating the hell out of Nancy in *Oliver Twist* he would often whistle *'Got to Pick a Pocket or Two'* to keep the mood balanced.

Unavoidable: *A Christmas Carol*. There is simply no way to miss seeing at least eight adaptations of this story every yuletide. It is no good saying 'Bah Humbug', you will end up watching every single Scrooge from Alastair Sim to Albert Finney and the surprisingly great Michael Caine in *The Muppet Christmas Carol*. (We are not surprised that Michael Caine was great, he always is, it's just that is extremely hard to act seriously opposite Gonzo the Great and Miss Piggy. Sir John Gielgud tried it once in an ill-conceived production of *The Muppet of Venice* and ended up trying to throttle Fozzie Bear during his 'The quality of mercy is not strained, *wokka wokka*' speech.)

Jane Austen

A superb writer, Jane Austen wrote all her novels in Bath, which must have meant her fingers got really pruney, but at least she was clean. So are her novels, which are safe to be studied at any high school. Austen's novels presented the world in 'a microcosm', which meant she rarely left the village and all her plots were the same.

This is an exaggeration, of course; in *Emma*, a strong-willed but too proud young woman realises she has made errors of the heart and marries nice Mr Knightley. Whereas in *Pride and Prejudice*, a strong-willed but too proud young woman realises she has made errors of the heart and marries the *secretly* nice Mr Darcy. These stand in marked contrast to Austen's final novel, *Persuasion*, where she was persuaded by her publisher to change the plot slightly by having the too proud young woman take seven whole years before she gives up and marries the nice Commander Wentworth.

Highly Recommended: *Pride and Prejudice*. A masterpiece. Benjamin Disraeli read this novel over 17 times. Presumably on purpose, we know the plots are similar, but Disraeli was no dum-dum and would realise that this wasn't *Emma* by at least Chapter Four. Although a wonderful book, one wonders about the harm it has done to the romantic life of many young women who wrongly believe that haughty, ill-tempered young men are *their* Mr Darcy, whose heart and true nature shall be revealed in due course. As Senior Ladies know, most young men like that are just rude bastards and the only thing revealed in due course is that they were secretly working their way through all your girlfriends. Jane Austen remained single her whole life; smart girl.

Approach with Caution: *Mansfield Park*. This is known in literary circles as Austen's 'problem novel', the problem being that the heroine of the book, Fanny Price, is such a miserable pill. Yes, there are lots of long metaphorical walks around walled gardens and the characters put on a play at great length, also metaphorical, but you secretly root for the villain of the novel, Miss Mary Crawford, who is great fun and does not spend her entire time lighting metaphorical fires like Fanny does every two chapters. *6/10 Austen, see me afterwards.*

The Brontë Sisters

There were at least three of them and Branwell used to dress up occasionally 'for fun' so let us put him down as a provisional fourth. The famous Brontë sisters, Charlotte, Emily and Zeppo, all lived together on the windswept Yorkshire moors, although Emily would sweep the moors with a broom occasionally if brooding visitors were expected. An exceptionally close and competitive family, each sister was expected to complete at least one masterpiece before they were even allowed to get tuberculosis by their father.

Highly Recommended: *Jane Eyre*. Not to be confused with Jane Austen, this is the Jane that actually got married, to Mr Rochester in this case. No, no *spoiler alert*, this book is 200 years old and you are approaching the century at an alarming pace yourself. Mr Rochester's first wife was mad and kept in the attic so that Mr Rochester could brood in peace and gradually fall in love with the Help, which *did* help with the brooding but made his wife even crosser.

Jane Eyre is a fever dream masterpiece, an astonishing feat of imagination and tragic memoir, but this does not change the fact that Jane was a *homewrecker*. We have our eye on you, Eyre, and do not be surprised if that love-rat Rochester tries to lock *you* up in the attic when *your* looks go, too.

Also Highly Recommended: *Wuthering Heights*. Also terrific, also features a dark, brooding hero who stalks the Moors called Heathcliff. The Brontë girls certainly had a type, didn't they? Perhaps if there was a little less broody stalking across windswept moors and a bit more staying in with a nice cup of tea and a sensible cardigan, at least one of them might have made it to pension age.

Anyway, the book has a happy ending when Kate Bush reads it and makes that peculiar video where she twirls unsteadily about in red taffeta looking like a ballerina with balance problems. Like tuberculosis, the song is very catchy, although we doubt Ms Bush ponied up any royalties to Branwell or whichever Brontë was left by this point.

Approach with Caution: *The Tenant Of Wildfell Hall*. Look, it's fine, but it's an Epistolary Novel, which basically means that the author can't be bothered with prose and does the whole thing with a series of suspiciously long letters. Jane Austen got away with this in *Sense and Sensibility*, but it is tougher sledding here and switches to diaries halfway through, which is even worse. If the Brontës were The Beatles, Anne was clearly the George of the group. This is the literary equivalent of one of those ponderous Indian songs that you would skip over so you could get to *'When I'm Sixty-Four'*. We advise the same here.

H. Rider Haggard

Although his name sounded like inappropriately familiar advice for the wedding night, Rider Haggard wrote extremely well in a 'Boys' Own Adventure' Style for Grown-Ups. In real life, Rider Haggard was a real adventurer and barrister (a rare combination indeed, most barristers regard selecting the Coconut Slice for morning tea as enough adventure for a whole week).

In his spare time Rider Haggard personally started the Boer War, in the hope of giving himself more material, which was a mistake as the whole war turned out to be a bore, except for Breaker Morant shooting prisoners while reciting poetry.

Highly Recommended: *King Solomon's Mines*, a roaring adventure which has been ripped off by *Indiana Jones, Jurassic Park* and every single film where somebody pauses and says, *'Listen... the drums have stopped'*. (With the exception of *'Let It Be'* where the drums stopped all the time because Paul and George kept arguing.)

The hero of *King Solomon's Mines* is Allan Quatermain (think Clint Eastwood but less femme), who follows a mysterious Secret Map to search for – as the title might slightly give away – King Solomon's Mines. Personally, we don't recall King Solomon as being much into mining from Sunday School; he was more concerned with telling two women they could cut their baby in half. (They didn't, it was a trick. The *real* mother was revealed when she broke down and begged King Solomon to put the child into day care because she needed some sleep.)

Also Recommended: *She*, another African adventure featuring the very sexy and mad Queen Ayesha or '*She Who Must Be Obeyed*' (yes, *that's* where it is from, not *Rumpole*). Rider Haggard was offered 100 pounds for the copyright for *She* but chose a 10% royalty instead. As the novel went on to sell, and yes this figure is right, 83 *million* copies in the next 75 years, we and Rider Haggard's incredibly wealthy heirs feel he made the right call.

Among the people who read *She* were both Sigmund Freud and Carl Jung who theorised a lot about women on the basis of this sexually sadistic fictional character. So did we, but we kept that sort of thing to ourselves and did not do it in front of patients.

F. Scott Fitzgerald

The most famous writer of 'The Jazz Age', although he wrote no Jazz whatsoever, unless you count '*Your Feet's Too Big*', which we don't, because Fats Waller wrote that. A handsome and charming fellow who was born into wealth and glamour, Scott Fitzgerald became a brilliant worldwide success after the publication of his first novel while he was still at Princeton. Naturally, he reacted to this ceaseless good fortune by slowly drinking himself to death.

Many people blame this rather odd reaction on his choice of wife, Zelda Fitzgerald, but then again she did have the same last name as him, so some kind of kismet seems to have been at work. Zelda was a very beautiful and talented flapper but she was also bonkers; she bonkered Ernest Hemingway amongst others, and spent most of her time either in a Loony Bin or being rather cruelly caricatured in her husband's novels; for instance in the...

Highly Recommended: *The Great Gatsby*. Like most of Scott Fitzgerald's novels, this book is about extremely rich people who, despite having everything, drink a lot and are miserable. (Wherever did he get his ideas from?) Jay Gatsby, the mysterious tragic hero of the novel, is a man desperately trying to repeat the past, which is also the business model for many channels on Foxtel. Jay says 'Old Sport' quite a lot, is obsessed with Zeld... we mean Daisy, his old love, and also throws giant, really cool parties that are supposed to be spiritually empty but sound like a lot of fun and we would definitely go if invited, Old Sport.

A wonderful novel that is also wonderfully short, *The Great Gatsby* is beloved by high school students for its lack of length, clear themes, obvious symbolism and a choice of Leonardo DiCaprio or Robert Redford for those who give up and decide to rent it instead.

Approach with Caution: *The Last Tycoon.* This was Scott Fitzgerald's last novel, unfinished because he kept deciding to finish a bottle of gin instead. Although people keep pretending that the ending *would* have been a humdinger, the two-thirds that is there is not terribly interesting.

What *is* interesting is that while writing this book, F. Scott and his latest gal pal would amuse themselves of an evening by going out onto their balcony and listening to the married couple next door fight. The wife was a very funny and sarcastic young actress, the husband was a very handsome and unfaithful young singer. That couple were Lucille Ball and Desi Arnaz, and many years later they turned this bickering into ten seasons of *I Love Lucy.* Told you it was interesting.

CHAPTER 30

Senior Moments in Dieting

EVERY NOW AND THEN YOUR DAMN G.P. WILL GIVE A SERIOUS *lowered voice talk* about your 'sedentary lifestyle', which is a polite way of saying it's time to lose all the chub, Butterball, and go on a diet.

Dieting used to be known as 'Slimming' or 'Reducing'. This was back when dieting was believed to be a temporary curse; now it is a lifestyle, an industry, a religion and the topic of at least 50% of the books stocked in Dymocks.

As Seniors we have the advantage of having lived through decades of the various smiling snake oil salesmen and confident con ladies trying to pass their latest gimmick off as *'A Diet Revolution'*, most of which proceed with the same success and stability of the French Revolution: initially full of wild promise and elation, inevitably ending with bitter despair and you taking a guillotine to a series of chocolate eclairs while doing the knitting.

With this exclusive *Senior Moments Diet Guide*, Dieting Seniors are advised to remember the following diets that have hoodwinked us in the past; feel free to avoid or re-embrace them as you please. (We both know you are not going to stick to your diet anyway, but, as the coroner [*Kenneth Williams*] said to the proctologist [*Hattie Jacques*] in '*Carry On Up the Lavatory*', let us go through the motions together.)

Calorie Counting: A simple diet where you calculated the calories consumed in every meal, added it to your height, forgot whether you wrote down Kilojoules or Calories, started again, divided it by the span of your attention, gave up and had a milkshake to make you feel better. *(426 calories with 2 scoops, 23% of recommended daily intake.)*

The diet worked if you had the self-control of the Dalai Lama and the math skills of a recent graduate from NASA. Neil Armstrong was the only person to ever accurately count his calories for over a month, although Buzz Aldrin claimed he used to sneak Space Food Sticks on the sly.

Weight Watchers: Very popular in the 1960's. You all had to join a special club and then once a week you gathered to sit around and watch each other gain weight. All food was allotted a certain number of 'points'; once you had reached your point limit you simply stopped filling in your Weight Watcher Book accurately so people wouldn't denounce you at the next meeting.

Weight Watchers were also first off the mark to sell an entire range of Weight Watchers food items for you to consume, an inherent conflict of interest you might think, especially as they won either way. The *Weight Watcher's Ice Cream* was particularly suspect in the 'mixed messages' department. It was delicious, would come in a small tub (which seemed unnecessarily sarcastic), complete with a tiny wooden spoon which you could use to spank yourself after you had wolfed down eight of the damn things.

The Grapefruit Diet: A very simple diet. Every morning you ate half a grapefruit. It was so dreadful you couldn't eat anything else for at least 24 hours. The other half of the grapefruit was then given to Jimmy Cagney who mashed it into a moll's face. (No, *not* a mole, that would have been cruel.)

The South Beach Diet: Go to the beach and walk south. Surprisingly effective, but a lot of Senior Dieters did tend to drown at High Tide.

Rationing: The original diet helpfully caused by Hitler in 1939. Worked wonders on the British for years, despite the fact they all became obsessed with sweets. Having half their teeth missing probably made them weigh less, so swings and roundabouts.

The Food Pyramid: Built by Ancient Egyptians, the food pyramid was carefully constructed to make the Pharaoh depressed because he was only allowed sweets, cake or chips 'very sparingly'. It is still a mystery to this day as to how the pyramid was built, especially on the bottom level, where you were allowed 6 to 11 servings of Rice or Pasta every day. (Why it was so important to eat at *exactly* 6 to 11 was never explained, surely 11.05 am would have been acceptable?)

Sadly, although worshipped through much of the '70s and '80s, the Food Pyramid was eventually ransacked by Howard Carter (played by Peter Cushing in the movie) and many of the serving groupings were lost to history. Probably for the best, having 2 to 3 servings of 'Dry Beans' everyday may have led to a thin life but not a happy one.

The Israeli Army Diet: Wonderfully effective and quite a smash in the 1970's but very time-consuming as you had to invade Palestine once every six weeks. I still feel guilty every time I eat Hummus.

The Atkins Diet: Extremely popular until Dr Atkins keeled over from a heart attack. (Look, to be fair, he was probably on the 5/2 Diet at the time; these things are fads.) Basic idea was you eat mountains of meat coated with butter and the pounds will melt away, just like the pound of butter does on the giant T-Bone you now have to chomp down for breakfast.

Atkins devotees viewed bread like a Vampire views garlic. Far more Anti-Bread than Pro-Meat, Atkins disciples blamed bread for pretty much everything including the assassination of the Archduke Franz Ferdinand. (*Gavrilo Princip big baguette eater.*)

The Atkins Diet puzzled Dieticians because, despite rigorous testing, it seemed to work. Dieticians are always suspicious of all diets that seem to work; we often wonder whether it's because they live in fear of being done out of gig. With no fads to '*tut tut*', Dieticians would be left inside empty offices muttering 'Diet and Exercise' to their bored secretaries. Serves them right, smug thin joyless sods.

Being a Rotten Cook: This was an excellent diet and very common before Keith Floyd, Jamie Oliver and MasterChef came along and ruined the low standard of gastronomy that had blessed most of us with a thin waistline. Now everybody can cook, even men, and you can see the results waddling past you in any shopping mall.

Low G.I. Diet: Very popular during WW2. Apparently, if you dated short US servicemen you would lose weight. Plus, they would give you chocolate and silk stockings if you promised to lose, or at least loosen, your virtue. The jitterbugging alone killed millions of calories, many WAACs lost a pound at a time if the band played the Gene Krupa version of '*Sing, Sing, Sing*'.

The Beverly Hills Diet: This was just plastic surgery and the occasional glass of freshly squeezed orange juice. The actresses who advocated this diet, Cher and Faye Dunaway among them, began to look freshly squeezed themselves after a while to the point of being unrecognisable.

The 5/2 Diet: Another piece of brilliance. For 5 days you eat like a pig and then for 2 days you starve yourself. Extending this principle worked out wonderfully for Karen Carpenter. Such a shame, she was one of the few drummers who could sing. Apart from Ringo, obviously, but she sang in key.

Keto: You remember, he was Inspector Clouseau's houseboy who would and could attack him at any time. The judo and the stress would lose you at least half a pound a week. The object of the diet is to reach 'Ketosis', which occurs when Keto stamps on your tosis. *Not now, Keto, you fool!*

Paleo Diet: Essentially the Atkins Diet but with a lot more talk about cavemen. Very big on nuts and berries, the 'science' of this diet is often enthusiastically explained by Handsome Chefs who seem to be missing a few berries upstairs and believe that *The Flintstones* was a documentary.

The CSIRO Diet: An extremely dangerous diet as it worked far too well. You would meet oddly familiar loose-skinned skeletons at ALDI only to realise that these were your former bridge partners, the Sandersons.

An unfortunate by-product of the CSIRO Diet is that everyone on it can *only* talk about the CSIRO Diet; all other conversation seems impossible. The CSIRO are studying the problem at the moment and hope to have a vaccine that will at least make adherents shut up for the duration of a dinner party. (Of course, when they are at the dinner party they won't even touch the slow-broiled Chicken Cacciatore you slaved over because *they are on the bloody CSIRO Diet, we KNOW!*)

Macrobiotic Diet: Eating only food entirely free of chemical preservatives in any part of its growth. Good luck with that. Strictly speaking, today I think you have two options left: honey found in a tree Winnie-the-Pooh style, and the odd coconut that might fall on your head. John Lennon and Yoko Ono were big evangelists for this diet in the 1970's and both *were* very thin, but they did add the extra secret ingredient of Heroin. Presumably the poppies were organically grown.

Jenny Craig: An obliging woman who would cook inedible food for you and drop it off at your house once a week. Seven indifferent choices each time, every time. Like eating in a bad restaurant in your own home, with not even the satisfaction of leaving an insultingly small tip as you already paid far too much for it well in advance. The diet did work, but you had to keep eating Jenny Craig's meals; once you ate good food your appetite unfortunately returned. This is what is known as a *'vicious circle'*, which is also the shape of your bottom once you give up Jenny Craig.

SlimFast: On this once-popular diet, you pretended that your jaw was broken and slurped solid-ish 'drinks' that contained meals. Like being an adult toddler. If you want to just drink and be thin, stick to Martinis. Betty Bacall did this her whole life and she looked fabulous, even at the end. Serious thought was given to making her a Lenin-style glass tomb just to make all the other Society Gals jealous, but due to her blood-alcohol level it was ruled unsafe by the New York Fire Department, a tribute to any Senior in itself.

The Scarsdale Diet: A smash hit book in 1978. Essentially the Atkins Diet with a different postcode, this diet became even more popular in 1980 for an exceptionally macabre reason. The author of the diet, a Dr Herman Tarnower, was murdered by his ex-lover, a Ms Jean Harris, who claimed that *she* had come up with the diet *and* ghost written his bestselling book.

Ms Harris got a 15-year sentence and no royalties but did look fabulous in vertical stripes so there was an upside. We are not saying that an ex-lover will necessarily murder you if you try the Scarsdale Diet, but unless you are a Senior with a blameless love life (yes, including Uni) we recommended skipping it to be on the safe side.

The 'All' Diets: i.e. eat all the potatoes/bacon/turkey/eggs you want but *only* eat potatoes/bacon, etc. These single ingredient diets always sounded like something dreamt up as a sort of second-rate *Grimm's Fairy Tale* curse; where Cinderella was doomed to eat all the lobster that she liked until she could fit into that ballgown. Well, not Cinderella, she had those mouse tailors that could whip up something flattering in moments, but you get the idea.

All of these 'All' diets All ended up in the same place: with you sitting on the lavatory waiting for All the constipation to be over. The one exception we will concede is the All Egg Diet; Paul Newman tried that in *Cool Hand Luke* and he never looked more handsome.

Smoking: Yes, we know it's not P.C., or probably even legal to say, but smoking *was* a sort of diet that made everyone look a) thin and b) supercool. Whenever they show you one of those old black and white panoramic photos in the paper of 'the crowd at Bondi Beach in 1958' and you marvel at how there is not a single tubby person there, do remember that it is actually a *colour* photo, the atomic plume of cigarette smoke just makes everything look black and white. Still, we did look gorgeous, didn't we? *Sigh.*

(Speed was also wonderful for dieting. It did drive many people insane and even Understanding Private G.P.s stopped prescribing it eventually, but you would not *believe* how spick and span the house used to look! And we played eight sets of tennis every day! How *did* we manage it? Oh that's right, we were on Speed.)

CHAPTER 31
Senior Memory Test

PLEASE ANSWER THE FOLLOWING QUESTIONS ABOUT THE PAST honestly and to the best of your ability. Answers may be written down and posted to *Senior Moments, 221B Baker St, London.* This is not actually our address, but we are far too busy to read our incoming mail in any case, as we keep telling the persistent fellows at The Tax Department and The Bailiff's Office. Anyway, pay attention and good luck:

1. Maralinga was:
    a.   That Argie soccer player who kept cheating
    b.   Not nearly as sexy as the Bikini Atoll
    c.   The biggest bomb Britain ever dropped here, unless you count Mick Jagger in *Ned Kelly*

2. What were (or was) Reds under the Beds?
    a.   A grave threat to the nation
    b.   The reason Ming kept winning
    c.   Lucille Ball and Ginger Rogers if you were Errol Flynn on a good night

3. Fine Cotton was:
    a.   Only available at David Jones until the '70s
    b.   A horse of a different colour
    c.   The only time a race in Australia was ever fixed, except for days that end with the letter 'y'

4. The Black Stump was located:
a.   Out the back of Burke
b.   Under the Black Bails
c.   Close to the station. Their prawns and bacon entrée was surprisingly tasty.

5. Pavlova was:
a.   A clever dog who could ring a bell
b.   Compulsory by law at any Australian social function until 1988
c.   Slightly more butch than Nureyev

6. The America's Cup was won because of:
a.   The winged keel
b.   John Bertrand
c.   The fact they hadn't locked up Bondy yet

Please check the box if you remember any of the following:

❑ **The Bogle-Chandler Mystery**
Although there are competing theories, to this day nobody is sure why any doctor would call voluntarily call themselves Bogle. Chandler of course went on to be everybody's favourite character on *Friends*.

❑ **The Magic Pudding**
Great book that showed what Norman Lindsay could do when he tried. Sadly, he wasted his life painting beautiful naked ladies and living in the Blue Mountains. Fool.

❑ **The Petrov Affair**
This incident shocked Australia and especially Mr Petrov who could never figure out who on earth Mrs Petrov was having

the affair with. A famous photo was taken which poignantly showed Mrs Petrov's despair when she was told that she would be flying back to Russia on Jetstar. At the next stop, Bob Menzies intervened and made Mrs Petrov get off the plane and live secretly in Adelaide with her husband for the rest of their lives. (Yes, it was a brutal punishment, but we did win the Cold War.)

❏ **Charles Sturt**
Famed explorer who made the remarkable discovery of a university in Bathurst, of all places. He spent three years there, but sadly made the mistake of getting a degree in 'Communications', which meant he was unemployable.

CHAPTER 32

Senior Moments in Television

THE MODERN SENIOR IS CONFRONTED BY A BEWILDERING ARRAY of modern Television choices, both when it comes to the TV sets themselves and the programmes that are 'streaming' from them. What was once a reliable evening of Boob Tube pleasure has now become like homework, as we dutifully slog our way through *The Wire*, *Peaky Blinders*, *Blindy Peakers* and any one of the 72 Grim Danish Detective Series that we are assured are great once you '*really get into them*' and '*understand the arc*'.

Like Noah, we are sick of arcs in general, and long for the days when TV consisted of Dramas we could understand without crib notes and that went for One Hour. (Except for the once-a-season exciting Two-Parter, which even then was a strain on the memory and the second week helpfully started with James Garner saying '*Previously, on The Rockford Files*'.)

Seniors can also remember a time when Sitcoms were *actually* comedies, not half-hour dramas in disguise that throw in one half-hearted ironic joke once every 15 minutes, if that. (Seriously, what has happened to sitcoms? They seem to be all sit and no com. Yes, we enjoyed *Fleabag* very much but are comedies supposed to make you cry and feel depressed? We can do that on our own *Fleabag*, cheer us up, for God's sake, like *Cheers* used to do. *Cheers* had an oddly depressing opening theme song but the rest of it was very funny. Personally, we blame the removal of the Live Studio Audience. Maybe the Live Studio Audience are still there and just feel depressed and quiet; we don't blame them.)

Things being what they are we advise all TV-Loving Seniors to take it easy on yourself and wallow in the cathode-ray produced nostalgia that is your Senior Right. Here are some suitable Senior Television Shows that will *not* let you down or at least won't let you down terribly in the final season finale, because they had *no* final season finales, they all just got cancelled.

Murder, She Wrote: This was a very rare show that actually starred a Senior who was indeed a star: Angela Lansbury. Angela played crime novelist Jessica Fletcher who lived in the bucolic Maine coastal town of Cabot Cove, where once a week one of her cheery neighbours would obligingly be murdered so Jessica could solve something.

Tom Bosley from *Happy Days* (the TV show, not the Samuel Beckett play, although he did have range) played the local Sheriff and quite frankly he was terrible at his job. The town's mortality rate was higher than that of London when Jack the Ripper was still roaming about in good nick.

Usually the people murdered were only visiting from other shows – for instance Frank Burns from *M*A*S*H* got poisoned in a diner and Tonto from *The Lone Ranger* was stabbed in his own swimming pool – but whatever way you looked at it, the Feds should have been called in halfway through the first season of the show at the latest.

The real mystery of the show is how Jessica ever got any of her books finished; the coroner spent less time examining corpses than she did. We suspect her editor did a lot of redrafting, or as much as he could before Eddie Albert guest starred and strangled him with his own typewriter ribbon. (Easier than you would think. We speak in the abstract, of course.)

Columbo: This was a brilliant show for any forgetful Senior because they showed you who did it straightaway and then Peter Falk would gradually work out what you *already knew* for the next 90 minutes. *Columbo* was a cat and mouse show, but unlike Tom and Jerry it was rarely intentionally hilarious.

Actually, *Columbo* was great all round, with terrific writing and acting and A-List guest murderers like Dick Van Dyke, Janet Leigh and even Johnny Cash, who usually only murdered the counter-melody. Robert Culp, Patrick McGoohan and Jack Cassidy were particularly good at murdering people and were allowed back to do it multiple times. (It did make one wonder about Lt. Columbo's detective skills however, as he never seemed to recognise them from the last time.)

One other thing we used to wonder about was Mrs Columbo. Although frequently mentioned by Lt. Columbo, we *never* actually saw her or even heard her voice and the, perhaps unworthy, thought has crossed our mind that Lt. Columbo may have murdered her. If so, we are sure he is tracking himself down, playing the long game, pretending to be a bewildered bumbler before turning around and saying 'Oh, just one more thing...' and then the *hammer shall fall*.

The Honeymooners: A wonderful comedy starring the Great One, Jackie Gleason, and the superb Art Carney. Although still hilarious, the fact that in every episode Ralph threatens to punch his wife in the face jars somewhat with modern sensibilities. '*One of these days, Alice, one of these days. Pow! Right to the Moon!*' Yes, Ralph never followed through on these battery promises, and we doubt if he could have even punched Alice out the window let alone into the Outer Atmosphere, but the threats themselves constitute assault and he would get at least three months today.

The Honeymooners is sadly unknown to the young, but it was shamelessly ripped off by *The Flintstones*, which in turn strongly influenced *The Simpsons*, so in a strange karmic way, every time you watch Homer Simpson strangling his son Bart, modern audiences are seeing the fulfilment of a domestic violence promise that has been a long time coming.

Perry Mason: Unlike *Ironside*, this was shot at a time when Raymond Burr was still thin enough to stand up. Perry Mason was a brilliant criminal defence lawyer who, with some leggy help from his secretary Della, would win *every single case*. Perry could have the Buddha in the stand, he would still make him crack up and confess to some fearful crime just before the last ad break.

The chap we felt sorry for was the Prosecuting Attorney, the hapless Hamilton Burger, who lost 271 cases in a row. Apart from the weekly pay cheque, why did he bother showing up? (Then again, this could be said of many careers including that of Raymond Burr's dietician.) The show ran for nine seasons and Raymond Burr did not run at all, hence his resorting to a wheelchair in *Ironside*.

Interestingly, the producers of *Perry Mason* invented a plot device called the 'Dumb Dora', which meant that in the last scene of every show, relaxing in his office, Perry would explain to Della *why* he had won the case, *how* he had figured it out, and *what* mistake the villain had made. This was so the theoretical Dumb Dora watching at home would not be confused about anything in the show. Patronising yes, but we wish that the producers of *The Wire* would think about reshooting many episodes using the 'Dumb Dora'. We are still only halfway through the second season and are so lost we are not sure if we might in fact be watching *Game of Thrones* by accident.

Funnily enough, although the phrase 'Dumb Dora' is obviously offensive, the only Dora we have ever seen on television was indeed an extremely stupid girl called Dora the Explorer, inexplicably popular with many Senior Grandchildren. Dora insisted on talking to us even though we couldn't answer back, and sang songs with her cheery friend 'The Map' that made the lyrics of The Wiggles sound like Stephen Sondheim by comparison. *'I'm the map, I'm the map, I'm the map, I'm the map'* went the entire lyrics of one such ditty, which was imaginatively entitled *'The Map'*. This song would be sung at least six times an episode as the tot next to us on the couch watched enthralled. It makes you wish Raymond Burr was still alive so we could bump off Dora and he could get us acquitted. Either that or he could sit on her.

***Rawhide*:** A great show with a great theme song. This show was so good that Clint Eastwood could only play the second lead. Each week the Rawhide gang would *'head 'em up, move 'em on, move 'em on, head 'em up'*, and invariably run into trouble with their doggies. (No, not Cocker Spaniels, this is what they called their cattle. We don't know why, either.) Eric Fleming pissed off Clint every week by starring instead of him as trail boss Gil Favor. *Why* have you never heard of Eric Fleming since? Well, this is a gruesome but interesting story.

In 1965, after eight years of *Rawhide*, Eric was offered the lead in a film called *A Fistful of Dollars* directed by an unknown Italian hack called Sergio Leone. He said no and instead went to Peru to make a film called *High Jungle* where an action scene he was filming in an Amazon river (never a good idea) went a *bit* wrong, to say the least.

Eric got caught in a current and his body turned up three days later half-eaten by piranhas. He was 41. Meanwhile, sloppy seconds Clint took the Sergio Leone offer, became and remained one of the biggest stars in the world and is still directing hit movies at the age of 89. The lesson is clear: make sure you carefully check the credentials of your Peruvian River Stunt Co-ordinator before anyone, especially the piranhas, yells 'Action!'

Rawhide also featured Sheb Wooley in a supporting role who, as every Senior should know, also wrote the immortal classic '*The Purple People Eater*'. (No, not on the show, in real life. As good as the *Rawhide* writers were, it would have been difficult to weave that one in as a campfire singalong.) God almighty the world has changed since *Rawhide* hit the air in 1957, possibly for the better when it comes to novelty songs.

The Dick Van Dyke Show: Still wonderfully funny today and worth watching for Laura Petrie wearing those capri pants alone. The fact that Dick Van Dyke is still alive cheers everybody up; he is wonderful and can be forgiven anything including his attempt at a cockney accent in *Mary Poppins*.

Back in the day, stars were not dummies, and despite the fact that Dick's character was called Rob Petrie, the show was named after him, ensuring he could not be fired. This same tactic was used by Mary Tyler Moore when she got her own show, called *The Mary Tyler Moore Show*.

This was not actually her name at the time, as in real life she had remarried TV producer Grant Tinker and legally her show should have been called *The Mary Tyler Tinker Show*. To make matters more, or slightly less, confusing, Mary played a character on her show whose first name was also Mary.

Ed Asner, whose name remains unchanged, was not so lucky when he spun off Tyler Tinker into his own show named *Lou Grant*, which somehow was no longer a comedy and may have started this whole modern rot of 'dramedy', a single word that ruined two genres at once. We do have another suspect, however…

M*A*S*H: This show began as a wonderfully funny, wisecracking comedy and then, 11 years later, ended up with Hawkeye having a nervous breakdown after ordering a Korean baby to be strangled on a bus in the middle of the night. (Not in real life or on purpose, but still, not exactly a hoot.) The finale of *M*A*S*H* was watched by a record 106 million people, all of whom thought the same two things: 1. *What the hell happened to* M*A*S*H? and 2. *I think Hotlips Houlihan has had a bit too much work done on her lips.*

At its best, *M*A*S*H* was the best: it could do comedy and drama brilliantly, but as the years wore on, and Alan Alda directed more and more episodes, unlike the Korean War itself, Dramedy was able to break the stalemate and declare victory.

Still, terrific stuff for the most part and 'Abysinnia, Henry' still makes us cry, especially when we think about all the terrible Disney movies McLean Stevenson had to do when his career didn't exactly pan out. Or maybe it did, maybe he *wanted* to be in a film called *The Cat From Outer Space*. Sigh. Poor Henry.

CHAPTER 33

Concluding Moments

AND SO, AS THE SUN SETS SLOWLY IN THE WEST (LOCATION dependent, we have no idea where you are standing. You could be an Astronaut for all we know – *yes, you could*; they let John Glenn back up there when he was 76), we wave goodbye as this *Senior Moments* book is drawing gradually to a close.

What have you learnt? Nothing, you are Seniors, you learnt everything a long time ago. The question was impudent in the first place and we apologise. We shall now leave you with some final '*Senior Moments*' to ponder upon as you wait for it to be early enough to have your first drink of the day without looking like an alcoholic. (Our tip: a moving LED placed strategically over the yardarm works wonders.) Good luck, stay Senior, and we shall see you in the next book.

It's a 'Senior Moment' when...

It's a Senior Moment when you stop worrying about becoming like your parents and start worrying about becoming like your grandparents.

It's a Senior Moment when you can't hum anything in the Top 40 but can still sing the entire opening theme to *Car 54, Where Are You?*

It's a Senior Moment when 'having a flutter' is something that sends you to the hospital instead of to the racecourse.

It's a Senior Moment when you watch *Dad's Army* and realise the entire cast is now younger than you. (On a good day you could possibly pass for John Le Mesurier's slightly older brother.)

It's a Senior Moment when it takes you longer to swallow the pills you have to eat before dinner than it does to eat dinner.

It's a Senior Moment when you remember when 'getting a snag' was something people did to their fishing line, not something they bought in a car park outside Bunnings.

It's a Senior Moment when you realise you will never be sexting. In fact, the closest you got was a handwritten note thanking someone for letting you get to second base.

It's a Senior Moment when your idea of an Apple technology breakthrough is fresh Granny Smiths in winter.

It's a Senior Moment when you remember when girls used to have to be on a pill to have sex and now you have to be on a pill to have sex.

It's a Senior Moment when you still call the ABC 'Channel 2'. (What happened to Channel 0, by the way?)

It's a Senior Moment when you think a 'Smart TV' means that it shows Max and 99 having a conversation with the Chief in the Cone of Silence.

It's a Senior Moment when your home phone rings and you answer it. (And you still have a phone, not a 'landline'.)

It's a Senior Moment when you still think of 'Shirley Temple' as a movie star, not as a drink option.

It's a Senior Moment when you stop flirting with Nurses to get their phone number and start flirting with them to get extra medication.

THE END

(stop reading now)

BACKWORDS by GILLIES MAX, MA

Stern. Hind. Abaft. Return. Spine. Vertebrae.

Best,
Gillies Max

ACKNOWLEDGEMENTS

Thank you to the editor of this book, Stacey Clair, for her infinite care and skill – I am in her debt. Not literally, she has a financial arrangement with Hachette for her editorial services and she has not yet won or even filed her much-promised lawsuit to 'show me'. I salute you Stacey and I hope that hell does indeed freeze over which would then obligate you to edit another of my books.

Thanks also to Louise Adler, the publisher brilliant enough to recognise my own brilliance. An easy feat you might imagine, and I agree, but you have got to suck up to your publisher – that's mostly what the Acknowledgements page is for.

A sincere thank you to the many thousands of Wise Seniors who have already purchased tickets to the comedy revue *Senior Moments*. Well done. You are the real heroes. If it were not for you this book would not exist, and you may all regard yourselves as co-authors (no royalty).

There are many who have urged me to use this work of literature to promote future productions of *Senior Moments*, coming soon to a theatre near you, but I have refused. This is despite the fact that critics have hailed *Senior Moments* as '*brilliantly witty*', '*a delight*' and '*a perfectly adequate way to spend 90 minutes of what remains of your life*'.

There are obviously many strong arguments that it would be a public good in this Acknowledgement to tell all Seniors to buy a ticket to *Senior Moments* as quickly as possible, especially as groups of 8 or more get special prices, but I will not debase myself to such naked hawking, I serve only the muse of literature. If, dear reader, you *want* to look at **SeniorMomentsShow.com.au** to see all upcoming dates, I cannot stop you. Well, I could but it would be very time consuming and I can't be bothered.

Thank you too to Archbishop Desmond Tutu.

Finally, I would also like to thank Tom Cruise, who I no longer blame for the death of our mutual friend Goose.

hachette
AUSTRALIA

If you would like to find out more about Hachette Australia,
our authors, upcoming events and new releases you can visit
our website or our social media channels:

hachette.com.au
HachetteAustralia
HachetteAus